FRAMING

The way to ensure summer . . . is to have it framed and
glazed in a comfortable room.

To William

FRAMING

Moyra Byford

SEARCH PRESS

First published in Great Britain 1996

Search Press Limited
Wellwood, North Farm Road,
Tunbridge Wells, Kent TN2 3DR

ISBN 0 85532 805 3

Printed in Spain by Elkar S. Coop, Bilbao 48012

CONTENTS

INTRODUCTION

A picture frame should be chosen and made with care so that it enhances the painting or object that it surrounds and is not so dominant that the eye rests on it instead of being led into the picture. It should harmonise with the rest of the presentation, be of pleasing proportions, and be of a width and substance that is appropriate to the size of the picture.

Paintings and artwork are not the only things that are framed; people often want to frame mementoes, pieces of craftwork and embroidery as well as collections of Victoriana, medals, thimbles, spoons or badges. Even three-dimensional items like baby's first shoe, decorated eggs and wedding bouquets can all be framed in order to be displayed. The advantage of framing is that these items can be viewed and yet kept safe, and, if the frame is glazed, kept free from dirt, dust and damage.

Initially frames were almost always made for paintings and were always made of wood, which was stained to simulate the panelled walls where the paintings hung. In the Baroque period heavy gold frames became a popular alternative, either made from plaster or composition built on to a wooden base, or from carved wood. The more ornate the frame, the better it fitted in with the rest of the surroundings.

The nineteenth century marked a period of change. Better frames were still hand-made, but mass-produced finishes began to creep in to make cheap frames for the mass-produced engravings that were so popular.

From the end of the nineteenth century frames began to be made from almost anything – perspex, metal, papier mâché, cardboard, velvet, silk, or paper – but most frames were still made from wood or had a wooden base. Wood was very versatile: it could be painted, gilded or stained; sawn into fretwork designs; and carved, shaped, moulded or embossed.

Now, at the end of the twentieth century, we have an enormous selection of wooden mouldings with a multitude of factory finishes for every possible use, and we can still add our own choice of colour on to bare-faced mouldings. Recently, in the interests of ecology, polystyrene-based mouldings have been introduced that have excellent finishes to simulate those available on wood.

However, with all these finishes most frames are still square or rectangular in shape and made from four pieces of picture-frame moulding with corners mitred at 45°. Most of the projects in this book use this basic shape, and I start you off with the simplest form of frame that does not require glazing.

But the moulding is but one part of the story. Whereas in the nineteenth century there was the option of two or three ivory or gold mountboards to choose from, now we have an almost overwhelming display, with several manufacturers vying with each other to produce more colours and textures. More importantly, there is also a choice between ordinary standard mountboard and conservation mountboard. The latter is acid-free and has been developed to help preserve the artwork within the frame and to prevent unsightly stains and marks occurring in later years. This conservation theme is carried through to tapes, adhesives and backings.

Once the basic skills of cutting mitres and assembling a frame have been mastered there are more options to be tried, and mount-cutting skills to be learned. Frames with mounts are usually glazed, and glass is essential for watercolours and other works of art on paper. The glass protects the work from dirt and the mount acts as a buffer to prevent it from touching and possibly sticking to the glass. A mount is particularly necessary around an elusive medium such as charcoal or pastel to prevent loose particles transferring on to the glass.

The combination of mount and glass is also suitable for a wide variety of other uses: for prints, photographs and other flat art and craft work.

For more three-dimensional craft work, multiple layers of mountboard can be assembled together to create depth. Alternatively, special frames can be made from deep-sided mouldings to contain, for example, a collection of medals, a paper sculpture or three-dimensional découpage.

I also show you how to make a number of other types of frame – a double-sided one for an old document, a box frame for a model boat and fancy frames that are made from four or more pieces of moulding mitred at various angles.

This nineteenth-century watercolour was last reframed in 1960 with a simple flat wooden frame. Since then the seal on the back has broken and it has suffered somewhat from the intrusion of wood smoke and nicotine. I used conservation-quality materials, a new sheet of glass and a gold frame to 'restore' the painting to its original state.

MATERIALS AND EQUIPMENT

When you start a new craft two factors have to be borne in mind – what materials and equipment are essential and where would be a suitable place to work. Obviously, it is best to have somewhere specific to work, preferably not too small an area, as wood mouldings can be up to 3m (10ft) long and are difficult to manipulate in a small space without damage. However, a long space such as a garage or garden shed can easily be adapted and I know many people who create beautiful work in converted outhouses. It is most important that the bench at which you stand to work should be of the correct height to avoid back strain, but this can easily be achieved by raising a table on wooden blocks. Try to have as large an area as possible, which is clean and dry, with more worktop space than you think you need – there never seems to be enough room.

A small selection of the hundreds of different shapes and sizes of finished-design mouldings that you can use to frame a picture.

Materials for making frames

To make a simple frame you will need a suitable length of moulding, a backing board, some glue, a few nails, some sealing tape, a couple of screw eyes and a length of picture cord or wire.

Mouldings

Picture moulding is sold in lengths which can vary considerably, but is priced by the metre (or foot). When calculating the length of moulding that you will need for a frame, remember that there will be wastage at each corner when it is cut. The total wastage is roughly equal to eight times the width of a moulding, and this amount must be added to the total picture size (see page 25) to give the minimum amount of moulding needed.

There is a vast array of ready-made finished designs available, which vary in width, price and quality – a small selection is shown on page 8. Most framers select a few designs within their price range and use them repeatedly, ringing the changes with different coloured mountboards. Artists use the same approach, sticking to a well-tried combination of colours that suits their palette. Different choices sometimes have to be made by craftspeople who need deep mouldings for particular purposes. The main objective is to choose a moulding that is not only going to complement your work, but is also strong enough for the size of the picture, whether it has glass or not.

Alternatively, you can buy **bare-faced** mouldings which are bare of any surface finish. They can be decorated by the framer using stain, paint or wax to make a unique finish. The advantage of using these mouldings is that the staining is done after the pieces are cut, thereby leaving a remnant of bare moulding which can be used for another frame and stained a different colour. This eliminates a lot of waste, which is always the enemy of the framer.

The profiles of mouldings also vary considerably and have names to describe them: some of the more common profiles are illustrated and named in the picture (right).

The inner edge, nearest to the picture, is called the **sight-edge**. The sight-edge is frequently painted gold to enhance the picture and this can be further accentuated by the use of a **slip**. A slip is a flat wooden gold or bare-faced insert which when cut with mitres at the corners forms an inner frame.

A consideration when choosing a moulding is the depth of the rebate, which must contain all that you wish to put into the frame. This is a point to watch because, curiously, some mouldings have incredibly small rebates. A moulding with a deep rebate at the side is called a **hockey stick**, and mouldings of this type are ideal for framing three-dimensional pieces of craftwork.

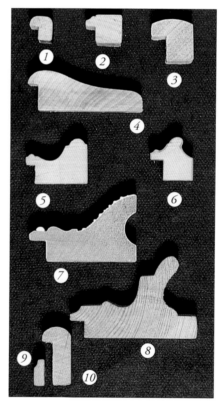

Some of the different profiles you can use.
1. Cushion
2. Flat
3. Deep
4. Reverse
5. Scoop
6. Shallow scoop
7. Spoon
8. Gothic
9. Slip
10. Hockey stick

Opposite
A selection of bare-faced mouldings and the stains, dyes and waxes that can be used to make one-off designs for your frame.

Backing board

Most frames need a board to keep the artwork clean and protected from the back, and to help keep the frame rigid. However, there are two exceptions: an oil painting on canvas, which has to be left open at the back so that the wedges can be hammered in from time to time, and any item which needs to be viewed from both sides.

Backing boards are usually cut from large thin sheets of MDF (medium density fibreboard) – 2mm ($^1/_8$in) is the thinnest available. MDF is preferable to ordinary hardboard as it is smooth on both sides.

Alternatively, you can buy ready-made strut-backs, which are backing boards that have a hinged leg on the back. They allow the frame to be self-standing and are used primarily with photographs.

Glue

One of the usual proprietary brands of wood glue is perfectly suitable for this type of work.

Sealing tape

The traditional way to seal the back of a picture is to use gummed brown-paper tape – it forms a perfect seal against dirt and insects and lasts for many years. It can be bought from good-quality stationers' shops.

Turn-buttons and kidney-plates

These come in various sizes and are used to secure strut-backs into frames.

Nails

Panel pins are used for fastening the corners of a frame: 13mm ($^1/_2$in) ones are best for small frames, 25mm (1in) for larger ones. However, if a project involves very large frames in wide mouldings you must use larger carpenters' nails. Although panel pins can also be used to secure the backing board in the frame, there are two tools that make the job easier (see page 15).

Screw-eyes, cords and wires

In order to hang the picture, screw-eyes are attached at the back of the frame, then either nylon cord or wire is threaded through the eyes and tied. The cord is usually tied straight across the back so that it is concealed when the picture is hung. However, the use of picture rails and picture hooks is becoming fashionable again and for this look the picture cord or chain has to be considerably longer.

Wreath-top hangers

These are decorative hangers used instead of screw-eyes and cords. They are fitted centrally at the top of the frame and allow it to hang flat against a wall.

From the top: Turn-buttons, kidney-plates and screws for use with strut-backs; steel and brass panel pins; screw-eyes and rings; wreath-top hangers; brass picture wire and cords.

Equipment for making frames

Recently, there has been a quiet revolution amongst manufacturers of framing equipment. There are now some excellent tools available at very competitive prices, designed specifically for the home framer to make well-cut joints at home.

You do not need a lot of equipment to get started in framing. For example, to make the first project in this book – a simple unglazed frame – you will only need a mitre saw, a band clamp, a good long ruler, a hammer and a craft knife. These basic tools are available in good tool shops and DIY stores. As your interest in framing grows you can gradually expand your toolbox to include other specialised pieces of equipment.

The mitre saw

Recent designs of mitre saws are very accurate and easy to use; the sawing action is so gentle that even a small person can use them with confidence. The saw blade is held on vertical bars within a framework so that it cannot rock from side to side when cutting. The framework is mounted on an integral protractor, pivoting about a central point, which allows the whole saw framework to be swung from side to side and locked in position.

The protractor is calibrated from a 45° position at the left-hand side, through 90° in the middle, and out to another 45° position at the right-hand side. Beneath the protractor there are notches to allow the saw to be locked at any angle. A number of saws include symbols to show the saw locking positions for cutting five-, six- or eight-sided frames.

Mitre blocks and tenon saws can be used for cutting mitres but, in the hands of anyone save the most experienced carpenter, they will give results far inferior to those obtained with a mitre saw.

Mitres saws might look expensive, but in fact they are quite cheap to buy.

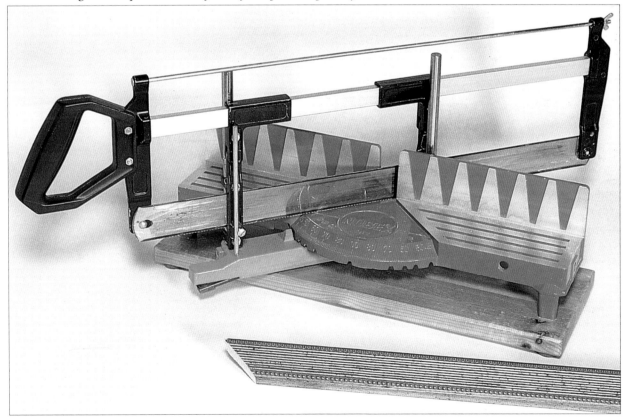

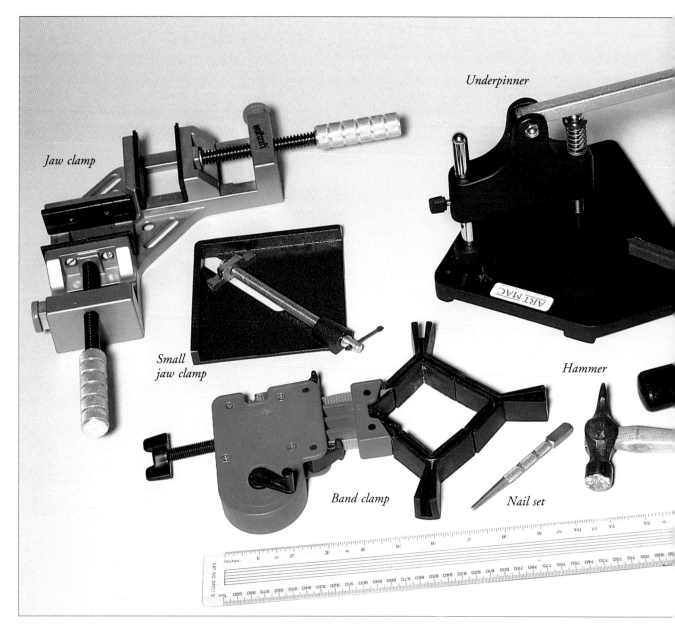

Jaw clamp

Underpinner

Small jaw clamp

Hammer

Band clamp

Nail set

Band clamp

The cut pieces of moulding need to be fixed together and there is a choice of equipment to make this a relatively simple task for the home picture framer.

A simple band clamp is the cheapest. This is a small plastic box from which a long continuous tape can be drawn. Small pre-formed plastic corners are threaded on to the tape and the four pieces of glued moulding are placed into these corners. The tape is tightened by means of a hand screw at its base, applying pressure to the four pieces of moulding and holding them firmly in place while the glue sets. The four corners have to be nailed as extra security when the glue is dry.

Jaw clamp

This is an alternative to the band clamp but it is a rather more expensive method of making a frame. Two pieces of glued moulding are placed carefully into the jaw clamp, which is tightened to squeeze them together. When they are firmly held the whole thing can be turned over and the joint fastened with an underpinner.

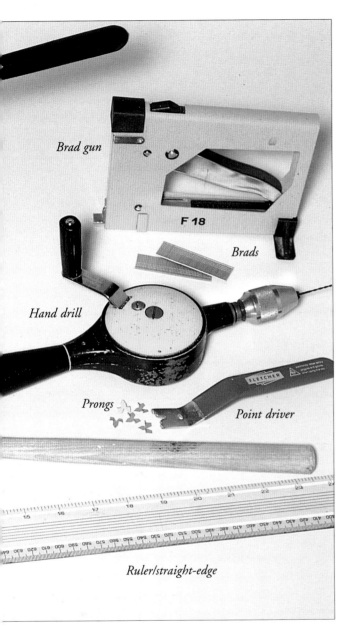

Brad gun

F 18

Brads

Hand drill

Prongs

Point driver

Ruler/straight-edge

profile mouldings up to 25mm (1in) wide. As each corner is dealt with individually it can mean that large frames made from wide mouldings are difficult to handle. Always insert a little glue before you put the pieces of moulding into the clamp to be on the safe side. An underpinner is not essential, but it is a nice addition to a workshop once you have got started and find that it can be justified.

Hammer
Choose a medium- to light-weight hammer; most jobs in picture framing are rather delicate and are unsuitable for a large carpenter's hammer.

Hand drill
Sometimes mouldings can be extremely hard and require a pilot hole to be drilled in each corner for the nails. A good hand drill is adequate and you will need a couple of fine bits.

Nail set
This small pencil-shaped piece of metal fits over the head of a nail and, with a tap from a hammer, is used to recess it. Fill the resultant hole to conceal it.

Ruler/straight-edge
Try to get a good steel ruler or a straight-edge that can be cut against, at least 1m (36in) long. Beware of aluminium ones because they can be damaged by a blade: you will need a ruler for every job you do, so it needs to be kept in good condition. The very best option is to have two: one clear plastic ruler and one steel straight-edge, both of the same length.

Point driver
You can use pins and a hammer to fix the backing board into the frame, but if you want a more speedy process you can buy this small tool which pushes sharp metallic prongs into the frame.

Brad gun
A brad gun is a little luxury which will really speed up the final assembly of a picture. Placed flat on the backing board and nudged against the rebate of the frame, it fires individual brads into the rebate by a squeeze on the trigger. The brads come in resined sticks which are loaded in the front of the gun.

Underpinner
Underpinners drive a small W-shaped metal wedge into the back of the corner across the mitred joint to hold it firmly in place. A hand underpinner is now available which enables the home framer to achieve results similar to those of the large commercial underpinners used by professional framers.

It does the same job as its automatic counterpart, but more slowly; each wedge has to be peeled off a strip and placed behind a magnetic rod before it is driven down into the back of the frame. However, it is effective and works very well on reasonably flat

Materials for making mounts

If you want to extend your skills to mount-cutting in order to frame watercolours, prints, calligraphy or any other flat crafts you will need to invest in some other materials and equipment.

The materials required to mount and assemble a watercolour, for example, consist of mountboard, glass and some sticky tape. Wherever possible try to obtain conservation-quality materials – standard materials contain acids which can intrude on and damage your painting or artwork.

Mountboard

The range of mountboards available is, I think, quite daunting and it is best to limit the colours that you use in order to avoid waste. Mountboards are sold in large sheets from which several mounts can be cut and it is advisable to consider carefully how the whole board could be used before buying an unusual colour for just one job. I find that a range of six to ten colours is more than adequate for everyday use and they can look quite different when used with a variety of mouldings.

In addition to the plain colours there are various textures which are attractive for specialist jobs; these include **flannel** and **cloud** textures. The latter has a pleasant mottled pastel appearance.

You can also buy a range of **coloured-core** boards which show a coloured line (including black) when the aperture is cut. This board can be used very effectively for some purposes, and I have included it in the projects on pages 36 and 42.

Many of the colours of mountboard are available in either standard or conservation quality. Conservation board is made from virgin pulp fibres which remain pure white for the life of the board, and the board contains no acid. Conservation board should be used for antique paintings and other items of value in order to protect them from the ugly stains and marks that can appear on paper.

Some of the range of coloured-core mountboards. From the top: grey with a blue core, white with a pink core, grey with a green core and grey cloud with a black core laid over a piece of blue cloud mountboard.

Glass

Mountboard marks extremely easily, so take great care when working with it to prevent fingermarks and other dirty marks appearing on the surface. Obviously it also needs protection when it is used in a frame, and this is traditionally provided by placing a sheet of 2mm ($^1/_8$in) glass in front of it, keeping the artwork and mount clean.

The easiest option is to get glass from your local supplier, who will cut individual sized pieces for you as you require them. This may cost a fraction more than cutting it yourself, but saves a great deal of aggravation. However, if you want to cut your own glass you will have to think about a storage area and a cutting table covered with soft fabric. There are many types of glass cutters but the best is one with a built-in oil reservoir which lays down a thin film of oil while cutting and makes the whole job easier.

Equipment for making mounts

There is a lot of equipment available for cutting mountboards, but you can start with a basic straight hand mount-cutter and then gradually add more items to your collection as you become more skilled.

Straight mount-cutters

A hand mount-cutter is the first essential: there are many makes available, but they all work on the basic principle of pushing a cutter along a line drawn on the back of the mountboard while holding it steady against a straight-edge. These are the cheapest of all the mount-cutters but they do take a little practice to learn. Other versions have the cutter mounted on an integral straight-edge, which helps to keep the whole thing steady. Have a good look at the cutters before you buy one, and choose a model on which you can actually see where the blade is cutting: this is vital to show you where to start and stop. Although this may seem a very fundamental piece of advice, not all hand mount-cutters are designed in this way.

There are other semi-professional mount-cutters that are easier to handle but, of course, they are more

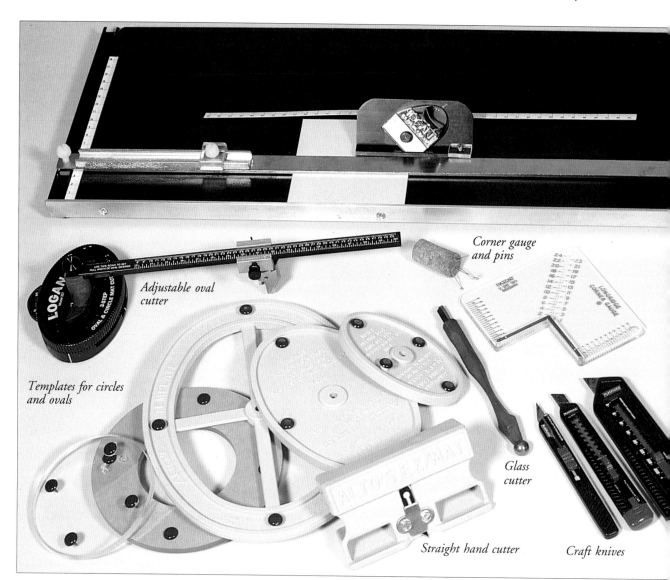

Adjustable oval cutter

Corner gauge and pins

Templates for circles and ovals

Glass cutter

Straight hand cutter

Craft knives

expensive. These usually have a baseboard to which a ruler is attached and have adjustments to alter the width of the borders to be cut. Sometimes the cutter is a separate item, sometimes it hooks on to and runs along the ruler. Obviously these cutters have a big advantage in terms of speed and accuracy, although you may still have to rule the borders on the back of the mountboard to act as guides.

Professional mount-cutters have stops which can be set to the required borders so there is no need to draw on the back of the mountboard. They do speed things up and they are a real luxury when cutting a whole set of mounts, but this type of cutter is not necessary when you are starting out.

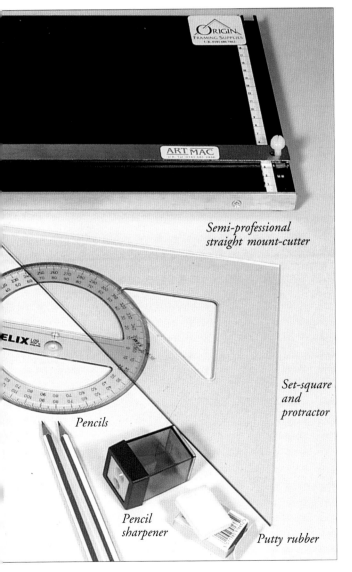

Semi-professional straight mount-cutter

Pencils

Pencil sharpener

Set-square and protractor

Putty rubber

Oval and circle mount-cutters

There is a small selection of oval and circle hand mount-cutters available which are quite easy to use and extend the range of subjects you can handle. They are not cheap, but they are invaluable if you wish to mount floral paintings, dried flowers, or other art and crafts that look more effective in ovals.

One type uses a series of templates which are secured to the mountboard with pins, following which you push a hand cutter round the edge. They need a little practice but they produce very good mounts at a reasonable price.

An alternative is an adjustable oval cutter. This is a more complicated device, but it does allow you to adjust the ratio between the height and the width of an oval. It is an effective piece of equipment which can add a great deal to your skills.

Craft knives

Craft knives that have retractable snap-off blades are the safest, and you always have a good sharp blade. These are used to cut the mountboard and MDF and for many other jobs in the workshop. It is also useful to have a small scalpel for delicate jobs.

Corner gauge

A corner gauge is essential if you want to rule lines around the aperture of a mount. It tucks into the corners of the aperture and has holes that can be marked through with either a pin or a pencil point.

Set-square and protractor

A set-square helps you cut mountboard with good square corners. A medium-sized clear plastic set-square is ideal for this purpose. A simple plastic protractor is also a useful addition to the toolbox.

Pencils and rubbers

Use sharp 2H or 3H pencils for marking out – soft pencils can smudge, and ball-point pens must be kept away from mountboard at all times.

Mountboard marks very easily and only a putty rubber should be used to clean it. These are available in art shops and they have the unique quality of disintegrating as they are used, so there is no danger of damaging the surface of the mountboard.

19

The finished oil-on-board painting in its frame together with some other examples of simple unglazed frames. Note the effect of a wide moulding on the small acrylic landscape.

BASIC TECHNIQUES

In this chapter I show you, stage-by-stage, how to make a simple unglazed frame. I then show you how to size mounts and how to use some of the mount-cutters that you can buy. These basic techniques are used for most of the other framing projects in this book with the notable exceptions of the box frame for a model boat (page 63) and the fancy cutting exercises on page 75.

Making a simple frame

You will need: a painting to be framed (mine measures 405 x 305mm (16 x 12in)); a length of moulding; a piece of MDF the same size as the painting; some 25mm (1in) panel pins; brown paper tape; two screw-eyes and a length of picture wire or cord. Choose a moulding that tones with the picture and is in proportion to the frame size. In this case I chose a 25mm (1in) wide pink-and-grey-washed moulding with a distressed finish and a gold sight-edge to tone with the blossom and the walls.

In this first project I am going to show you how to make an unglazed frame suitable for this oil-on-board painting. The same techniques can be used to make a notice board and to frame a mirror.

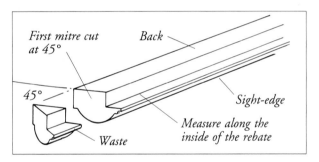

Stage one
Calculate the sizes of the cut lengths of moulding. Always measure along the inside edge of the rebate and include a small amount of 'ease', usually 2mm (^{1}/$_8$in), to allow the picture to slip easily into the finished frame. For this painting, cut the two long lengths of moulding to 407mm (16^1/$_8$in) and the two short ones to 307mm (12^1/$_8$in).

Framer's tip: When calculating the length of moulding you will need, remember that there will be wastage at each corner when it is cut. The total wastage is roughly equal to eight times the width of a moulding: add this amount to the total picture size to give the minimum amount of moulding needed.

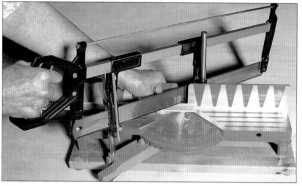

Stage two.

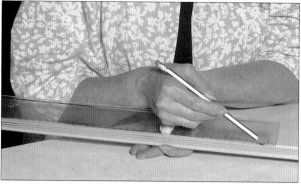

Stage three.

Stage two

Lock the saw at the left-hand 45° position. Lift the saw blade, insert the moulding from the left and push it flat against the backplate and down against the base of the saw, with the sight-edge facing you. Hold the moulding tightly in your left hand, lower the blade gently on to it, and draw the saw back and forwards to make the first cut.

Stage three

Measure 407mm (16$\frac{1}{8}$in) along the inside of the rebate from the edge which you have just cut and make a small pencil mark.

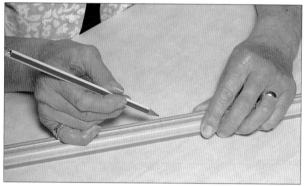

Stage four.

Stage four

Transfer this mark round and on to the top of the moulding to a point directly above the corner of the rebate. This will act as a guide for your next cut.

Stage five

Lock the saw in the right-hand 45° position. Insert the moulding from the left until the mark made in stage four is directly under the saw blade. Lower the saw blade on to it and make the second cut.

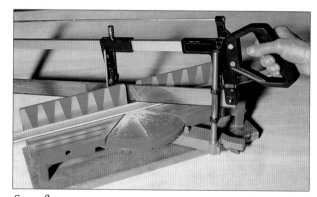

Stage five.

Stage six

Repeat stage two for the second long length. Now lay your first length (the master) back to back against the moulding, mark off the full length and then cut the second mitre. Cut the two 307mm (12$\frac{1}{8}$in) sides in a similar way.

> **Framer's Tip:** *Most framers cut the long sides of the frame first in case they make a mistake in the measurement, for then the pieces can be cut down to make short sides and there will be less waste.*

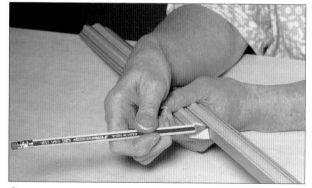

Stage six.

Stage seven

Take the band clamp, pull out a length of band sufficient to enclose the frame and thread on three plastic corners. Insert all four pieces of moulding and take up the slack (but do not tighten), adjusting the plastic corner pieces as you go. This may take a little time to master because the tape will want to spring back on its own. Remove one short length at a time, spread a little glue on both ends and then replace it in the clamp. Tighten the band, making sure that all four corners are in position and that the frame is square at each corner. When it is really tight the band twangs when you flick it. Wipe off any excess glue and leave it to set for about two hours.

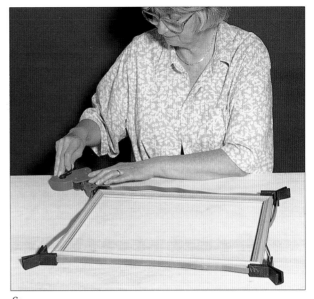

Stage seven.

Stage eight

For extra strength, nail the corners using 25mm (1in) panel pins and a small hammer. Nail one side of each corner, checking that you are nailing with the grain and turning the frame as you go.

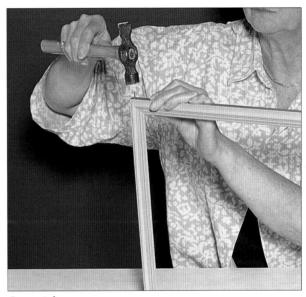

Stage eight.

Stage nine

Cut a piece of MDF the same size as the painting – 405 x 305mm (16 x 12in) – using your straight-edge and craft knife. The easiest way to do this is to score along the line three times and then break the board against the edge of a table: press down then up and the board will crack along the scored line. Tidy up the edges with a little sandpaper.

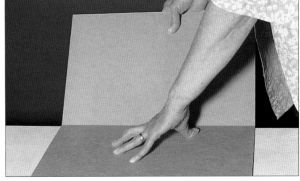

Stage nine.

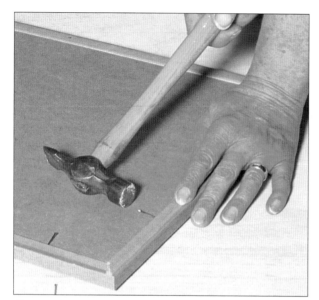

Stage ten.

Stage ten
Place the frame face down on to your worktable and then insert the picture with the backing board on top. Hammer 25mm (1in) panel pins into the rebate of the frame, flat against the backing board, so that they hold everything tightly in place. Place three pins equally spaced on the long side and two on the short side.

Stage eleven.

Stage eleven
Tear off four pieces of gummed brown paper tape a little longer than the sides of the frame and dampen them on a wet sponge. Place them neatly on the back of the frame a little way in from the edge so that they cover the join and the nails and cross over in the corners. When the tape is dry (in about an hour), trim off the corners with your craft knife.

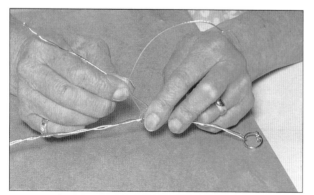

Stage twelve.

Stage twelve
Fix a screw-eye a third of the way down each side in the centre of the moulding and screw them in up to the hilt for safety. It is easier if you start the hole with a bradawl before you try to screw them in. Cut a length of picture wire slightly longer than twice the width of the picture, thread it through the two rings, twist the wire back over itself and make a neat join.

Alternatively, thread nylon picture cord through the screw-eyes and use it double, tying the knot to one side to avoid it fouling the picture hook on the wall.

Sizing mounts

The widths of the borders around the image area, and the subsequent 'total picture size' (i.e. the size of the picture and its mount) should be worked out carefully.

When deciding on the width of the borders, remember that some of the border will be hidden under the rebate of the moulding. Similarly, a small amount of the picture will be hidden under the mount when it is fastened behind the aperture. This is known as the 'tuck'.

My way of measuring the total picture size is shown in the diagrams below. For this exercise, I am using 50mm (2in) borders at the top and sides, and a 60mm (2³/₈in) border at the bottom.

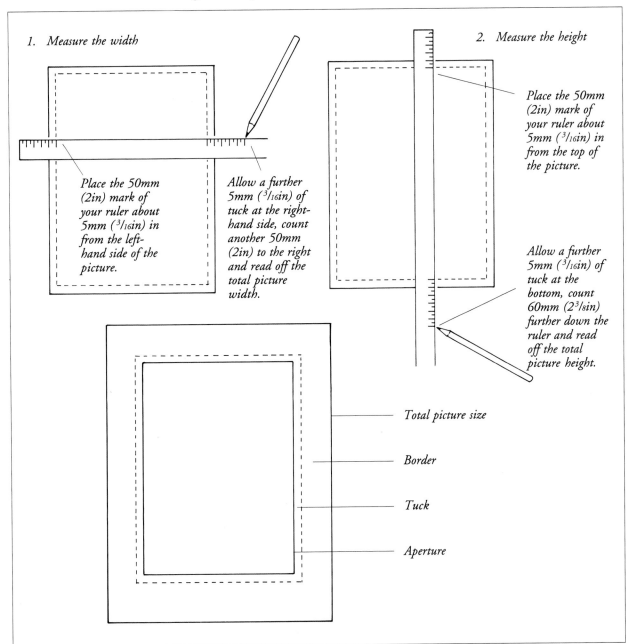

1. Measure the width

Place the 50mm (2in) mark of your ruler about 5mm (³/₁₆in) in from the left-hand side of the picture.

Allow a further 5mm (³/₁₆in) of tuck at the right-hand side, count another 50mm (2in) to the right and read off the total picture width.

2. Measure the height

Place the 50mm (2in) mark of your ruler about 5mm (³/₁₆in) in from the top of the picture.

Allow a further 5mm (³/₁₆in) of tuck at the bottom, count 60mm (2³/₈in) further down the ruler and read off the total picture height.

Total picture size

Border

Tuck

Aperture

The proportions of borders relative to the size of the subject to be mounted are most important. On contemporary pieces it is quite acceptable to have equal borders all round, but it is traditional to have a slightly wider border at the bottom than at the top and sides, which should be the same width. There is a theory that a wider border at the bottom prevents the painting from looking as though it is falling out of the bottom of the frame, but in this day and age anything goes, and framers are constantly experimenting with new ideas.

The size of the borders is all largely a matter of personal choice and taste, but certain rules of thumb do apply. A small picture usually has a mount with a fairly narrow border, say 30mm ($1^1/_4$in), with a larger picture having a mount with borders of up to 100mm (4in), especially if they are going to be decorated. However, it is always nice to break the rules and a tiny picture can look absolutely stunning with a wide border, although large pictures rarely look good with narrow borders because it makes the presentation look rather mean.

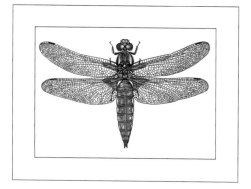

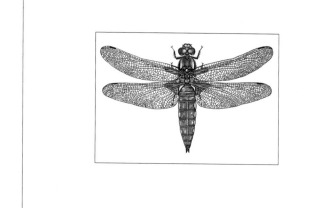

Proportion is all-important. Equal borders all round (top left), a wide border at bottom (top right) and wide borders on a small picture (right) are all acceptable. Compare these with the very narrow border (above), which is not very pleasing to the eye.

Using a straight hand mount-cutter

In this first mount-cutting project I am going to use a hand mount-cutter to mount a simple print with 25mm (1in) equal borders all round.

Choose the colour of the mountboard to tone with the colours in the print. In this case, I wanted to make the flowers stand out so I chose a blue-grey that toned with the background.

You will need: a small print (mine measures 150 x 115mm (6 x 4¹/₂in) and a piece of mountboard. You will also need some masking/conservation tape to fix the print to the mount.

Stage one
Allowing for a small amount of tuck beneath the mountboard and a 25mm (1in) border all round, the total picture size will be 190 x 150mm (7¹/₂ x 6in). Mark out these measurements economically on a piece of mountboard to avoid waste. Use your set-square to check that the corners are correct.

Stage two
With your craft knife and straight-edge, carefully cut out the piece of board.

Stage three
On the reverse side of the board, measure and mark the 25mm (1in) borders on all four sides, crossing the lines at the corners to make it obvious where to start and stop your cuts.

Stage four

Position your straight-edge on the outside of one of the lines and parallel to it. Holding the hand cutter firmly, dig the blade in just before the point where the lines cross at the corner, adjust your straight-edge so that the cutter will run along the line accurately, and push the cutter firmly until you get just past the cross at the other end. Now cut the other three sides and the centre of the board (the 'fall-out') should come away cleanly.

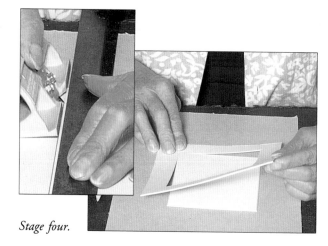
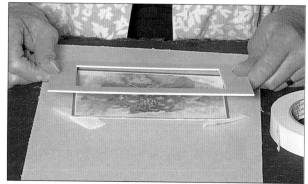

Stage four.

Stage five

Lay the print face up on a table and slip two pieces of masking or conservation tape (sticky side up) under the artwork, diagonally across each of the two top corners. Gently lower the mount on to the print, checking that the position is correct, and then press firmly on the top corners. Carefully turn the assembly over and apply more tape to the sides and the other corners. (The finished picture is shown on page 31.)

Stage five.

Using an adjustable straight mount-cutter

Landscapes, such as this watercolour, usually look much better when the mount has equal borders at the top and sides and a wider border at the bottom. I want to have rather large borders to allow space for ruling some lines around the aperture of the mount to lead the eye into the picture, so I have decided on 60mm (2³/₈in) borders at the top and sides and a 70mm (2³/₄in) one at the bottom. For this project I am using a semi-professional adjustable mount-cutter. I am also introducing the corner gauge to help draw in the lines around the aperture.

Allowing for the borders and for 10mm (³/₈in) tuck in both directions, the total picture size is 375 x 490mm (14³/₄ x 19³/₈in). Referring to pages 25 and 27, cut the mountboard to this size.

You will need a watercolour painting (mine measures 255 x 380mm (10 x 15in), a piece of mountboard, some masking/conservation tape and a fine-point fibre-tipped pen.

Stage one
Set the gauges for the bottom bar of the mount-cutter to 70mm (2³/₄in).

Stage two
Now set the two side stops to 60mm (2³/₈in).

Stage three
Tuck the mountboard under the bottom bar, face down, making sure that it is square and straight. Nudge the cutter up to one of the side stops, insert the blade and steadily push the blade along the bar until you reach the stop at the other end. You have now cut the bottom border. Most cutters can be either pushed or pulled, which gives a choice if you are left-handed.

Remove the board, alter the bottom bar settings (see stage one) to 60mm (2³/₈in), insert the board upside down and cut the top border.

Remove the board again, and leaving the bottom bar and left-hand stop at 60mm (2³/₈in), set the right-hand stop to 70mm (2³/₄in) as at stage two. Turn the mountboard so that the bottom border is nudged against the right-hand stop, which you have just altered, and cut the first side border.

Remove the board once more, alter the right-hand stop back to 60mm (2³/₈in) and change the left-hand stop to 70mm (2³/₄in). Finally, reinsert the board, make the last cut and the fall-out should come away cleanly.

Stage four
Tuck your corner gauge into the corners of the aperture and then, using a small pin, lightly prick marks, 5mm (¹/₄in) in, on to the mountboard

Stage five
Place a ruler face down to avoid blotting and draw lines with a fibre-tipped pen to join these marks.

Fix the painting to the back of the mountboard as described on page 28. The finished mounted picture is shown on page 31.

Stage one.

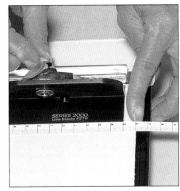
Stage two.

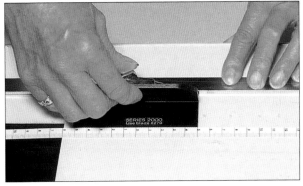
Stage three.

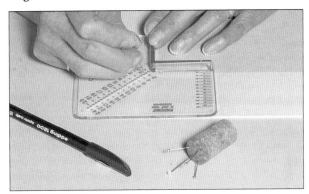
Stage four.

Stage five.

Using an oval mount-cutter

Oval apertures can be used to good effect with small items of craftwork, and in this project I am going to use an adjustable oval cutter to mount a little piece of lacework. Ovals also work well with some photographic portraits (see page 39). You can also cut ovals and circles using templates and a hand cutter (see page 42).

After measuring the items I settled for 30mm (1¹/₄in) borders all round, an oval aperure of 140 x 90mm (5¹/₂ x 3¹/₂in) and a total picture size of 200 x 150mm (8 x 6in). Having cut the mountboard to size, mark the exact centre on the front of it by halving the measurements and then drawing very light pencil marks, in the form of a cross.

You will need a small piece of craftwork, some mountboard and some double-sided tape. I find it a good idea to hold the art/craftwork against different coloured mountboards to find the most pleasing combination. For this example I chose the two shades of green.

Stage one

Adjust the oval size differential set in the base of the cutter to 50mm (2in) – the difference between the two measurements of the oval. Set the cutting head on the arm to 140mm (5¹/₂in) – the longest measurement. Press the small pins underneath the base unit firmly into the mountboard, aligning it over the pencilled cross.

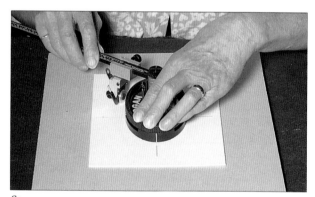

Stage one.

Stage two

The blade has three positions, which are adjusted by a small lever. Insert the blade and set the lever to position 1. Then rotate the blade right round and score the surface of the mount.

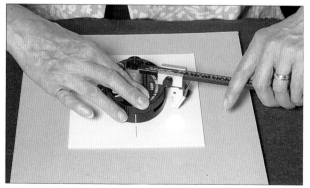

Stage two.

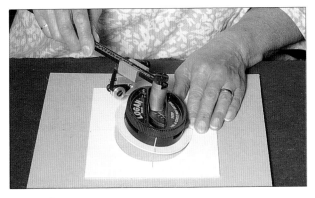

Stage three

Move the lever to position 2 and rotate the blade again; on this second circuit the blade digs a little deeper. Move the lever to position 3 and make a third cut, pressing a little harder. Now lift the cutter and the fall-out should come away with it.

Stage four

Fasten the craftwork with double-sided tape cut into tiny pieces so that they will not show; using this method the lace can be removed again, if necessary, without damage.

Proportion is all-important. Note how the border dimensions suit the subject and its size.

When you have learned the basic techniques of making frames and cutting mounts, you can combine these skills to frame a wide variety of subjects.

COMBINING TECHNIQUES

Now that you have learned the basics of making a frame and cutting mounts it is possible to combine these skills to frame a wide variety of items. In the following pages I will show you how to deal with photographs, pastels, quilling, sets of small images, canvas work and fabrics, three-dimensional objects, a model boat and a document that needs to be viewed from both sides. Finally I show you how to make a group of non-rectangular (fancy) frames for a set of pressed and mounted flowers.

Ways with photographs

One of the most popular things that people want to have framed are photographs. These can be seen in almost every home, and with a little imagination they can be framed in a more interesting way than is usually seen.

Any photograph that you treasure will be complemented by mounting and framing, and in this chapter I show you how to deal with various types of photographs.

Black and white photographs need individual treatment and when they are used with black-core mountboard, which shows a black line when the bevel is cut, the striking images in the photograph are complemented.

Small informal family snaps (especially those with unwanted backgrounds) will be enhanced by a mount, as will those old sepia photographs of your ancestors.

Framing a school portrait

Probably the most popular photograph is the school portrait, which is commonly taken against a blue background and presented in a dark-brown folder with an oval aperture. Getting away from this standard presentation makes the photograph look more interesting and gives it more individuality.

In this school photograph, in which the girl is wearing bright blue and the background is also blue, I chose a pale-blue mountboard with moderate-width borders, and decided to include a gold line round the aperture. If the subject is wearing a tie or badge you could choose a colour to tone with that.

To tone with the line and to lighten the whole picture I picked a 20mm (^{3}/4in) wide gold moulding.

The aperture can be rectangular or oval, depending on the shape of the head within the picture. In this case I feel that a good proportion is a rectangular aperture with a gold line drawn around it, so I have opted for 40mm (1^1/2in) borders all round. Allowing for these border and for a small amount of tuck, the total picture size is 315 x 255mm (12^1/4 x 9^7/8in). Cut the mountboard to this size and then cut out the aperture.

Referring to page 29, draw gold lines round the aperture, 5mm (^{1}/4in) in from the edge. Fasten the photograph into the mount using masking tape.

Cut the four pieces of moulding as described on page 22, allowing 2mm (^{1}/8in) for ease, and make up the frame. In this project I am using an underpinner for the corner joints (see below).

For this exercise you will need a photograph, a piece of mountboard, some moulding, a fine gold marker pen, an MDF backing board and a sheet of glass. For a free-standing picture use a strutback (instead of plain MDF) and secure it in place with turn-buttons and kidney-plates.

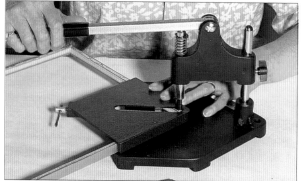

Using an underpinner to secure the corners of the frame.

Now cut a piece of MDF and a sheet of glass to the same dimensions as the mountboard. Lay the frame face down on the worktable. Clean the glass and place it in the frame, followed by the mounted photograph and the backing board. Do not delay while doing this, because dust particles can become trapped between the glass and the mount.

You can now fasten the sandwich in place using a hammer and nails. Alternatively you could use a point driver or a brad gun as shown opposite. Seal the gap with four pieces of wet gummed brown paper tape, crossing them at the corners. When these are dry and tight on the back, use your craft knife to trim the excess off the corners.

> *Framer's Tip: Before you start to saw your moulding, it is a good idea to double-check your measurements to avoid making any mistakes. They should of course be accurate, but errors can happen.*

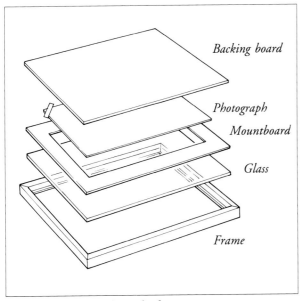

Backing board

Photograph

Mountboard

Glass

Frame

Assemble the 'sandwich' in the frame.

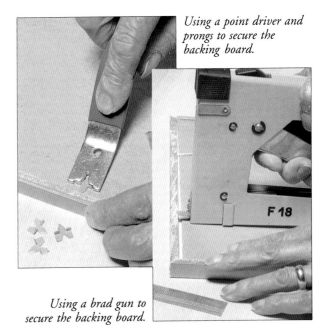

Using a point driver and prongs to secure the backing board.

Using a brad gun to secure the backing board.

Using a strut-back

If you want to have a free-standing frame you can use a strut-back instead of plain MDF. These can be purchased in standard sizes and can be made from cardboard or MDF (MDF is stronger and longer-lasting). If you want to change the picture in the frame from time to time, you can use kidney-plates and turn-buttons to fasten the strut-back. However, I personally feel that this method weakens the back and I prefer to fasten and seal the strut-back the same way as as I do with MDF – changing a photograph really only takes a few minutes with the proper equipment.

Position a kidney-plate across each of the top corners of the frame and use small brass panel pins to fix it in place.

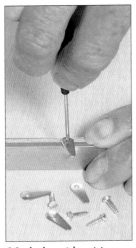

Mark the mid position on the two sides and the bottom of the frame, and then screw in a turn-button centrally in the width of the moulding.

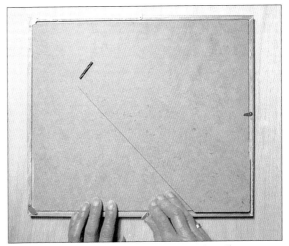

Assemble the sandwich and secure it in place by turning the legs of the turn-buttons round on to the strut-back.

Black and white photograph

For this black and white photograph of reflections, I decided not to introduce any other colour. For the mount, I chose a white mountboard with a black core, and for the frame a narrow black moulding. I want to have a 5mm ($^1/_4$in) white border between the edge of the photograph and the black core line of the mount-board, so I will be gluing the photograph to a slightly larger piece of white textured paper.

Spread PVA adhesive sparingly on the back of the photograph, taking care not to get any on the top surface. Position the photograph on the textured white paper with a border all round and leave to dry.

Decide on an aperture size by measuring the photograph (including the small white border). For this size of picture I suggest 40mm ($1^1/_2$in) borders at the top and sides and a 55mm ($2^1/_8$in) border at the bottom. When you add these measurements to the aperture, the total picture size is 355 x 265mm ($14^1/_8$ x $10^1/_2$in).

Mark these measurements economically on your mountboard, cut out the board and cut the borders. Attach four pieces of double-sided tape to the white paper (outside the white border area). Now carefully lower the mount on to the white paper, checking that the borders around the photograph are even, and then press firmly into place.

Cut the MDF and glass the same size as the mountboard, make up the frame, and then assemble and seal the sandwich in the usual way.

You will need a black and white photograph, a piece of textured white paper (big enough to allow a 5mm ($^1/_4$in) white border all round plus some more space for the tuck), PVA adhesive, a piece of black-cored white mountboard and a narrow black moulding. You will also need some MDF and a sheet of glass.

Spread a layer of PVA on to the back of the photograph, turn it over and lay it down on to a piece of white textured paper. Use a soft cloth to ensure a good contact all over.

Use pieces of double-sided tape to secure the mountboard on to the mounted photograph.

Informal family snapshot

When choosing a mountboard to tone with a photograph, look at the background colours to guide you in your choice. Pale greens and blues harmonise well with skies and greenery, allowing the subject of the photograph to stand out. Before you make your choice try various colours against your photograph to see how much difference they make. One colour of mountboard will probably look better than any other and that is the one you should choose.

For this small 150 x 100 (6 x 4in) snapshot I have decided to emphasise the green tones by using a green mountboard and frame (made from bare-faced moulding stained with water-based wood dyes).

I decided on narrow borders of 30mm ($1^1/4$in) all round, which, after allowing for tuck, made the total picture size 205 x 155mm ($8^1/4$ x $6^1/4$in). Cut the mountboard, MDF and glass to size. Cut out the aperture and then fasten the photograph behind it.

Cut four lengths of moulding, allowing for the usual 2mm ($^1/8$in) of ease. Using a wad of cotton wool dipped into apple-green wood dye, stain the mouldings and then set them aside. When they are perfectly dry, stain again using lavender wood dye – use a cotton-wool bud to get into the grooves. Do not apply too much of this second colour; the aim is to retain a green shimmer through the lavender. When the mouldings are dry, make up the frame in the normal way and assemble and seal the sandwich.

To frame this family snapshot you will need some mountboard (try out various colours and use the one that looks best), a length of bare-faced moulding and some water-based wood dyes, a piece of MDF and a sheet of glass.

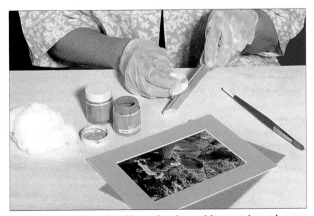

First coat each length of bare-faced moulding with apple-green wood dye and set aside to dry.

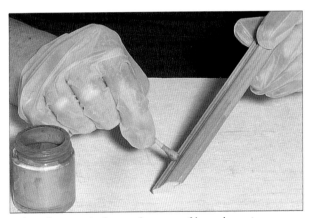

When the green is dry, apply a coat of lavender, using a cotton-wool bud to get into the grooves.

Old sepia photograph

Old photographs usually look good when set in oval mounts and this 1920s portrait is no exception: an oval aperture complements the curves in the hair-style and the sweater. Study portraits carefully and arrange the aperture to give more space in front of the face than behind the head. This 'looking space' prevents the face from looking cramped against the edge of the mount.

Take care when choosing the colour of mount-board as white or ivory could make the photograph look dirty. Here, the light parchment mountboard and limed ash moulding tone with the background shade of the photograph.

Apart from the usual mounting and framing materials, you will need some liming wax (applied with wire wool) and some clear wax (applied with a soft cloth) to treat the bare-faced moulding.

The oval aperture is 180 x 120mm (7 x 4³/₄in), which, with 40mm (1¹/₂in) borders at the top and sides and a 50mm (2in) one at the bottom, make the total picture size 270 x 200mm (10¹/₂ x 7³/₄in). Cut the mountboard, MDF and glass to this size.

Cut the aperture in a similar way to that shown on page 30, marking your cross on the mountboard 10mm (³/₈in) higher than the centre. Set the oval size differential to 60mm (2³/₈in) and the cutting head on the arm to 180mm (7in). Fasten the photograph behind the aperture.

Cut the lengths of bare-faced ash moulding, allowing 2mm (¹/₈in) of ease. Take up some liming wax on a piece of wire wool and apply a generous coat to each length of moulding, rubbing the liming wax into the grain of the wood. When you have coated the fourth piece, immediately start to remove the liming wax from the first piece with a soft cloth dipped into clear wax, rubbing until there is a sheen on the surface of the moulding and the liming wax only remains in the grain. Once the four pieces have been treated in this way you can make up the frame and assemble the picture as usual.

Apply a generous coat of liming wax, rubbing it well into the grain.

When you have limed the fourth piece of moulding, wipe off the liming wax with clear wax.

Compare the difference between the limed moulding and the original bare-faced version.

The four finished projects and a couple of other subjects in progress.

Multiple mounts

If two pieces of mountboard of the same size have borders of different widths cut in them you can get an interesting effect by placing them together. Two different colours can be used, but two mounts of the same colour are also surprisingly effective.

Double mounts are useful in certain circumstances, such as when you want to frame pastels or charcoal drawings, where it is necessary to keep the glass away from the image. However, you do not have to stop at two layers: three or even more layers of mountboard can be assembled and used to frame shallow three-dimensional pieces of craftwork such as quilling, beadwork, collage and parchment craft.

In this chapter I have included two projects. In the first project I show you how to prepare a double mount for a small pastel drawing, and then dye a bare-faced moulding to match the colour scheme. In the second one I use the multiple-mount technique, with apertures in concentric circles, to mount a small piece of quilling. In this project I also show you how to customise the mount by painting the sight-edges of the mountboard.

For the pastel drawing, I used a 25mm (1in) wide bare-faced moulding that I then coloured with rose pastel wood dye. For the mount I chose pale-pink and beige mountboards to reflect the tones in the pastel drawing.

The piece of quilling (made up from blue and gold paper) was mounted on a piece of orange mountboard. I decided to accentuate the blue by framing it in a deep-rebate, bare-faced moulding, painted with dark-blue acrylic paint. In order to keep the work away from the glass, I had to use four layers of mountboard and I chose a combination of the colours in the quilling.

Pastel in a double mount

Unlike watercolours and prints, pastel drawings must be held away from the glass: the particles are not always fixed, so it is essential to use a double mount when framing them, to stop the particles from getting on to the glass.

For this picture I have chosen to complement the colours in the drawing by using a pale-pink mount over a beige one, with a 10mm (^{3}/8in) overlap. The mounts are held together with double-sided tape. Stick a small piece of tape on each side of the lower mount (the 'inner'), well back from the cut edge, peel off the protective paper and place the 'outer' or top layer of mountboard carefully in position.

> *Framer's Tip: Double-sided tape is very sticky, so it is important to get the mounts aligned correctly first time, with the borders precisely the same width, especially with a multiple mount. You have only one chance to get it right and the effect is spoilt if the borders are uneven.*

You must take great care when assembling double mounts to ensure that the apertures are square with each other and that the visible border is equal all round.

I have also used a bare-faced moulding stained with a rose pastel water-based wood dye which again complements the colours in the picture. The dye is applied using a wad of cotton wool; use one single coat or, if a darker shade is desired, build up the colour with more coats. Two or more colours can be laid on one another to produce different effects, mixing either two pastel shades or a pastel and a wood shade. Infinite variations can be produced and I find it a good idea to experiment on offcuts of moulding.

> *Framer's Tip: Note that a double mount means that there is an extra 2mm (^{1}/8in) to be contained within the rebate of the moulding, which must be taken into consideration when choosing it.*

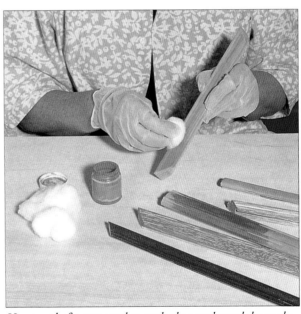

Use a wad of cotton wool to apply the pastel wood dye to the moulding. As you collect offcuts of mouldings you can experiment by staining them with different combinations of colours for future reference.

Quilling in a multiple mount

This piece of quilling, which is mounted on a piece of orange mountboard, measures 100 x 80mm (4 x 3¹/₈in) and I decided to fit it into a circle to echo the circular coils in the design. The circles are cut using a hand mount-cutter and a circle template.

The depth of the quilling means that four layers of mountboard are needed and I have chosen colours that reflect those of the quilling paper, which has one edge tipped with gold. Cut one 245mm (9⁵/₈in) square piece of blue mountboard and trim the other pieces to squares. Align a ruler from corner to corner and draw two diagonal lines to form a small cross in the middle of each piece.

Stage one
Align the template over the cross on the blue board and cut a 110mm (4¹/₄in) diameter circle.

Stage two
Insert a spacer in the cutter and then cut a 115mm (4¹/₂in) diameter circle on the gold square. Repeat this stage, using increasingly larger spacers to cut circles of 120 and 125mm (4³/₄ and 5in) respectively on the orange and the other blue board.

Stage three
Carefully paint the sight-edge of the inner blue, the gold and the orange mounts using the fine brush and gold acrylic paint, taking care that the paint does not spread on to the surface of the mounts. Mix an exact match of blue in acrylic paint and use this to paint the sight-edge of the outer blue mount.

Stage four
Starting with the inner blue mountboard, stick four small pieces of double-sided tape on each side near the outside edge. Position the gold mountboard over it, and, when you are satisfied that the borders are equal, press it down. Repeat the process with the orange and then the outer blue mounts. Finally, fix pieces of masking tape under the corners of the quilling, lay it face up on the table and lower the assembled mount over the top. Turn the whole thing over and add more tape if necessary.

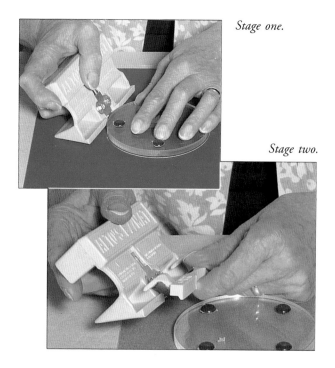

Stage one.

Stage two.

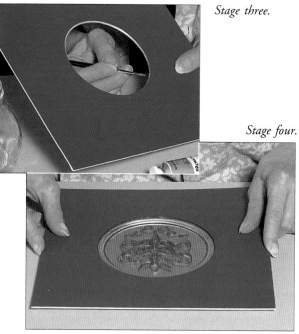

Stage three.

Stage four.

Cut four pieces from a deep-rebate bare-faced moulding, paint them with a dark blue paint, and, when they are dry, make up the frame as usual. Clean the glass, then assemble and seal the picture.

The completed projects and a framed piece of parchment craft. Normally, parchment craft would only need a single mount, but in this instance, where there are two separate pieces of work, a double mount is used to good effect, with the lacework part sandwiched between two mountboards.

Multiple-aperture mounts

Not only do multiple apertures in a single mount look very effective, but they also draw together a series of items which would be too small to frame individually. Family photographs are ideal for framing with multiple apertures but there are lots of subjects you can present in this way. The arrangement of the images can be either symmetrical or asymmetrical so long as it creates an interesting balance.

For the stage-by stage project I have chosen to mount a collection of old cigarette silks illustrating regimental flags. The flags are all much the same size and shape and need a symmetrical layout.

The other exercise is a mounted set of cards showing scenes from a Suffolk town. Here, there are two landscape-format and two portrait-format cards and so an asymmetrical layout is best.

There is an abundance of colour in this set of flags so I have used an ivory mountboard and mahogany-stained moulding with gold sight-edge. To complete the project you will also need some MDF and a sheet of glass.

For this arrangement of cards I needed to link two different colour schemes and I did this by using a blue-cored white mountboard together with a toning stain on the moulding. In this picture the prints are actually lying on the blue-coloured back of the mountboard Again you will need a piece of MDF and a sheet of glass to complete the framing.

Symmetrical set of silk flags

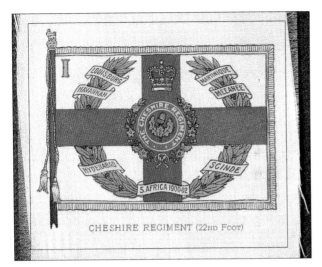

Stage one
First, measure each flag and decide on the size of aperture in which they can all be mounted. For these the aperture size is 70 x 60mm (2³/₄ x 2³/₈in) – the rectangle drawn on this flag.

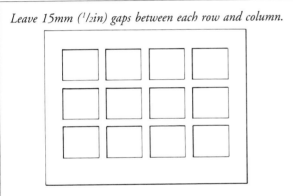

Leave 15mm (¹/₂in) gaps between each row and column.

Add 35mm (1¹/₂in) borders at the top and sides, and a 50mm (2in) one at the bottom.

Stage two
Draw a plan of the layout. Here, I decided on a symmetrical pattern – three rows of four columns with equal gaps between them. I also decided on equal borders at the top and sides and a deeper one at the bottom. I felt that this plan fitted the regimental subject-matter. Adding up the measurements (both horizontally and vertically) gives a total picture size of 395 x 295 (15¹/₂ x 11⁵/₈in). Cut the mountboard, backing board and glass to these measurements.

Stage three
Carefully draw the twelve rectangles on the back of your mountboard, making sure that all the lines are parallel and square. Take a little time doing this and recheck your dimensions.

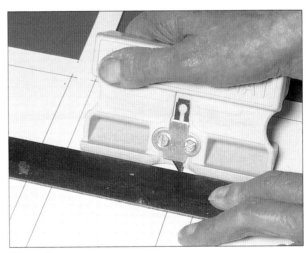

Stage four
Still working on the back of the mountboard, cut out the rectangles, making sure that you turn the mountboard after each cut so that the bevel edges face the correct way from the front. The first time you cut a multiple-aperture mount it is probably best to cut out each rectangle individually to avoid mistakes.

Stage five

Gently stretch and fasten each silk flag behind its aperture using masking tape: take care to ensure that the flag designs are exactly square and parallel to the edge of the apertures.

When the mounting process is complete, cut the moulding, allowing 2mm ($^1/_8$in) ease, make up the frame and assemble as usual.

The completed project.

Set of greetings cards

This set of greetings cards has two landscape-format and two portrait-format cards, and is an ideal subject for use with an asymmetrical multi-aperture mount. By alternating the landscape and portrait formats it is possible to create a pleasing square arrangement within the outer borders with a space in the middle for a title aperture to be placed.

When drawing your layout on the back of the mountboard, remember that the landscape and portrait shapes will be reversed. I have placed the larger portrait-format cards top left and bottom right, so on the reverse side these will need to be marked out on top right and bottom left. The remaining spaces are taken up by the two landscapes-format cards.

I used a coloured-core mountboard that has a white front surface and a blue core. The core appears as a blue border around each aperture and links the two colour schemes of the prints.

I cut the apertures and mounted the cards as I did the silk flags. I then used a bare-faced moulding for the frame which I dyed with a mixture of blue acrylic paint and wood dye.

Canvas work and fabrics

All fabrics have to be perfectly flat before they are framed, which means that they must be ironed and then held firmly in place within the frame to stop them cockling or creasing in the future.

Pieces of canvas work become very distorted while they are being stitched, even if they are worked on a frame, and need special treatment to get them flat. There are various patent devices available to help to stretch them, but I find that the good old-fashioned method of pinning out and steaming is the most effective. You will need a good solid board – a drawing board or piece of block board is ideal – which is considerably larger than the canvas work.

Other fabrics need to be ironed, but should be treated according to their type. It is best to be careful and use an iron set at a low temperature to start with, slightly increasing the temperature if necessary until all the creases are removed. The most difficult fabrics to get flat are those with some embroidered areas and some plain, as the embroidery seems to pucker around the edges and this puckering is often difficult to remove. Fabrics decorated with beads should be ironed with care through a cloth or alternatively on the wrong side, and fabrics with sequins should always be ironed on the wrong side with a cool iron as sequins melt very easily.

Beware of washing embroidered fabrics in case the embroidery silks are not colour-fast.

If the surface of the fabric is dirty it can be lightly rubbed with a putty rubber (obtainable from art shops), or with some fuller's earth. Do not rub fabric with bread-crumbs as modern bread contains a considerable amount of fat.

Some framers recommend that canvas work and other types of fabric should left unglazed. However, I do not agree with this view because, unlike oil paintings, which have a protective varnish, fabric will quickly become dirty and possibly plucked. If the piece of work is very dark in colour it may be desirable to use non-reflective glass rather than the normal picture variety.

In this chapter I am going to show you how to frame a simple canvas-work landscape, and then how to reframe a pair of old samplers.

For the canvas work you will need a deep-rebate moulding (I chose a gold one for this landscape), two pieces of MDF and a sheet of glass. To prepare the work for framing you will also want an iron, an old tea towel and some drawing pins.

For the samplers you will also need the iron and tea towel to flatten them but use dressmaker's pins (not drawing pins) to square them up on a piece of cardboard. You will also want some mountboard (I have used white for the background and dark red for the actual mount), some bare-faced moulding and some clear wax.

Canvas-work landscape

Canvas work tends to distort in the making, so before framing a completed work you must stretch it square and steam it perfectly flat.

Stage one
Using drawing pins, start at one corner of the work and pin 20mm (³/₄in) away from the stitched edge at regular intervals along one side, keeping it absolutely straight and parallel to the edge of the board. It is helpful to use a ruler to make sure that this first line is square and straight.

Stage two
Next, pin down one of the sides at right angles to the first, stretching the canvas slightly and pulling where necessary to make sure that the corner is exactly square to the original – a set-square will help you at this stage.

Stage three
By now you may well have some diagonal folds across the work, but ignore these and start to pin the third side, starting at the other corner of your original pinned line. You may have to pull the canvas quite hard to get this side square and straight, but it is extremely important that it is again at right angles to the original.

Now pin the last side in place and check the diagonal measurements across opposite corners – if the corners are square, these should be the same.

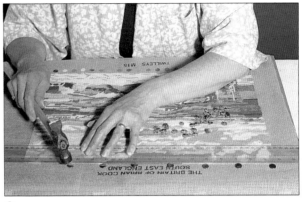

Stage one.

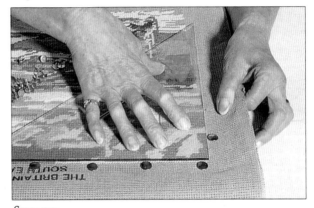

Stage two.

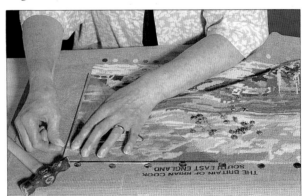

Stage three.

Stage four

Take an old soft tea towel or other similar piece of cotton fabric and soak it in water. Wring it out a little and place it over the canvas work so that the moisture soaks into the canvas. Place a hot iron, set for *cotton* or *steam*, on each section of the canvas for a few seconds – do not rub it back and forth in the usual ironing motion as this could iron in folds. By this time the piece should be completely saturated and steaming, but if there are still some creases the process can be repeated, again through the cloth. Alternatively, if you are using a steam iron, the final steam can be done without the cloth but with the iron held about 25mm (1in) above the surface of the canvas work so that the steam puffs through.

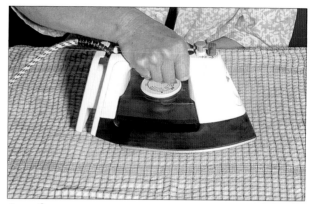

Stage four.

Set the board with the canvas work pinned on it aside to dry completely; this will probably take at least twenty-four hours – possibly longer. When it is absolutely dry, remove the drawing pins and you should find that the canvas is a perfect rectangle.

Stage five

Cut one piece of backing board to the exact size of the stitched area of the canvas work. In this case the measurements are 450 x 298mm (17³/₄ x 11³/₄in). Place the work face down on the table and position the board over the stitched area. The borders of the canvas can now be folded and taped on to the board with wide masking tape, folding the corners carefully so that they lie flat. It is necessary to pull the borders gently as you do this, taking care that you do not distort the stitched rectangle.

Alternatively, fasten the canvas on the backing board with a needle and strong thread. Fasten the thread in one corner, take it across the width of the piece and make another stitch on the other side, pulling the thread taut across the back of the board. Work down the length of the work; the stitches can be quite spread apart and zigzagged across the back. When the first two opposite sides are secure, fold in the corners neatly (make them as flat as possible) and stitch the other two sides in a similar way.

Now measure the overall size of the canvas and then cut the glass and a second piece of backing board to this size. Cut the moulding, allowing extra ease (2mm (¹/₈in)), and make up the frame in the normal way.

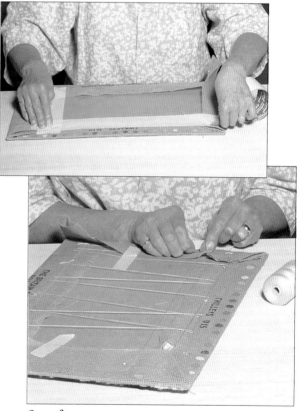

Stage five.

Auntie Maud's samplers

This pair of samplers dates from 1903. They were given to me to reframe still in their 1960s frames and mounts. The samplers had been mounted on dark-red and blue silk respectively, both of which showed through the weave of the canvas, darkening the whole effect and making the lettering very difficult to read. Simply removing the samplers from these coloured backgrounds and laying them on to white mountboard improved them immensely – the fabric looked cleaner and the lettering became legible.

Some of the stitching is made with a red thread, so I have chosen a combination of dark-red mounts, to tone with the red threads, and plain wooden frames to contrast with the texture of the canvas.

The hemmed edges of each sampler – which had been painstakingly worked by an eleven-year-old girl – are an integral part of the work, so I decided to set the aperture of the mount back from the edge of the samplers by 10mm (³/₈in) to allow the hemmed edges to show. The two samplers are different sizes, one being square and the other landscape format. I wanted both frames to be the same size and this meant that I had to have equal borders all round one piece and a deeper bottom border on the other.

Preparing the samplers

Lay the samplers face up on pieces of stiff cardboard and, using dressmaker's pins, pin them down on to the boards, pulling and measuring them until you are satisfied that they are precisely square. Iron them as described on page 50, then set them aside to dry.

Stick them down on to the white mountboard using tiny slivers of double-sided tape under the thick hemmed edges. You will get the best results if you stick pieces of tape in each corner and then at regular intervals of, say, 40mm (1¹/₂in) along each side; this should prevent the item sagging when it is behind the glass. Gently pull and stretch the sampler as you stick it on to the mountboard – this will also help prevent sagging.

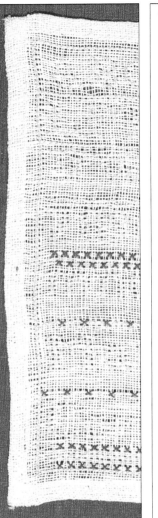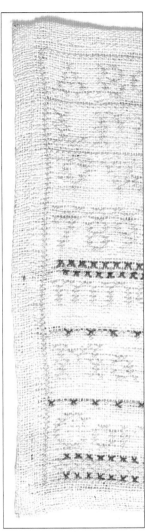

Simply changing the colour of the background greatly enhances the legibility of this old sampler.

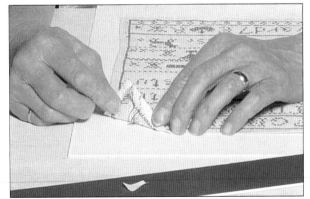

Use double-sided tape to fix the sampler to the mountboard.

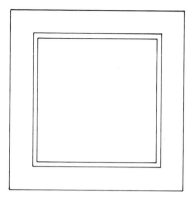

The large sampler is 265mm (10³/₈in) square. Allowing for a 10mm (³/₈in) white border all round (to show the hemmed edges) and a 50mm (2in) mountboard border on all four sides, the total picture size is 385mm (15¹/₈in) square.

Lay the mount over the sampler and make tiny guide marks with a very sharp pencil.

The landscape-format sampler measures 216 x 257mm (8¹/₂ x 10¹/₈in). Using the same total picture size, and allowing for a 10mm (³/₈in) white border all round, the borders are 54mm (2¹/₈in) wide at the top and sides and 95mm (3³/₄in) at the bottom.

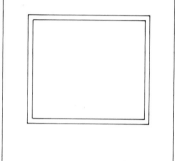

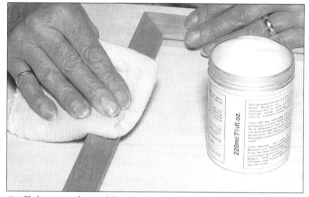

Buff the waxed moulding with a soft cloth to create a sheen.

Mounting and framing

When each sampler is firmly in place on its backing board, measure the length and width of each. Working with the square one first, decide on a total picture size that allows for a small white border and equal mountboard borders on all four sides. In this case it is 385mm (15¹/₈in). Both samplers are going to be in the same size of frame, so work backwards from the total picture size to arrive at the border widths for the landscape-format sampler. This must have a deep bottom border.

Cut two pieces each of dark-red mountboard, backing board and glass 385mm (15¹/₈in) square. Draw the borders on the reverse sides of the two mountboards, then cut out the two apertures.

Lay the mounts over their respective samplers, positioning them so that there is an equal border all round, and then make tiny guide marks with a very sharp pencil to help you position the mount again. Remove the mount and attach pieces of double-sided tape to the white mountboard, well back from your guide marks on each side.

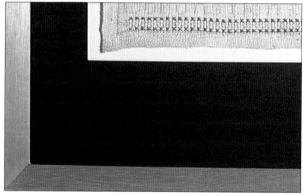

Detail of the finished landscape-format sampler with a deep bottom border.

Carefully lower the red mount over the sampler, aligning it with the guide marks. When it is in the right position press firmly on the double-sided tape.

Cut two sets of moulding, allowing 2mm (¹/₈in) ease, and coat each piece with clear wax: allow the wax to rest for a few minutes and then rub each piece with a soft cloth to create a light sheen. Make up the frames in the usual way and assemble the pictures.

One of the reframed samplers and the framed piece of canvas work.

Holding the glass away from the work

When framing items that are quite deep you must hold the glass away from the work by means of a plain insert of wood called a fillet. It is also necessary to have a **hockey-stick** moulding, or one with a very deep rebate. Mouldings are available with a range of rebate depths to accommodate anything from three-dimensional embroidery to a clock, and fillets are made in a variety of depths, in either gold or plain ramin, which can be stained.

To illustrate how to make frames of this type I have chosen a piece of hand-made-paper sculpture with a three-dimensional form that requires a fairly wide fillet in gold to tone with the gold threads and embellishments in the paper.

For this project you will need a three-dimensional object such as this paper sculpture, a sheet of mountboard, a hockey-stick, or deep-rebate moulding (with a rebate of at least 25mm (1in)), and a 15mm (⁵/₈in) deep fillet. You will also need some PVA adhesive, a piece of MDF and a sheet of glass.

Three-dimensional paper sculpture

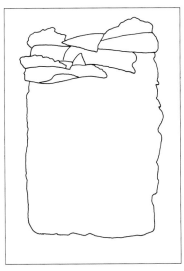

Measure the object and decide on the borders.

For this roughly rectangular shape I allowed for nominal borders of 25mm (1in) at the top and sides and a 30mm (1³/₁₆in) one at the bottom.

The total picture size is 305 x 200mm (12 x 8in).

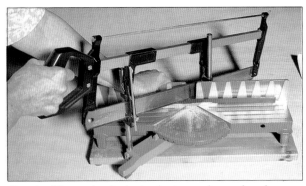

Cut the fillet so that its back edge is exactly equal to the internal length of the rebate in the made-up frame.

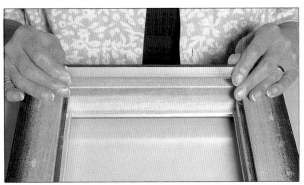

Insert the fillet so that it rests on the glass and fills one side.

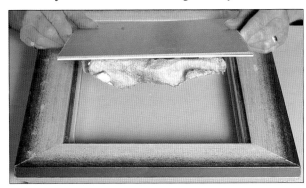

Place the paper sculpture with mountboard and backing board in position, resting on the fillet all round.

Measure the paper sculpture and allow for equal borders at the top and sides, and a slightly deeper border at the bottom. The total picture size is 305 x 200mm (12 x 8in), so cut the mountboard, backing board and glass to these measurements.

Spread PVA glue on one side of the backing board, align the mountboard over it and press firmly in position. Cover with a piece of clean paper and a board, place some weights on top and allow to dry.

When the mountboard is dry, stick the paper sculpture directly on to the front of the mount-board, allowing for the chosen borders.

Cut the moulding, allowing 2mm (¹/₈in) ease, and make up the frame as usual. Now insert the gold fillet upright in the mitre saw with its gold face pointing away from you and make a 45° cut across the end. Turn the saw blade to the left-hand side and cut the other end of the fillet so that the back edge of the fillet is exactly equal to the internal length of the rebate in the made-up frame. Cut four sides.

Lay the frame face down on the table, clean the glass and place it in the frame. Spread wood glue sparingly on the back and the mitred ends of one piece of fillet and carefully insert it in the frame so that it is resting on the glass and fills one side. Repeat this process immediately with the other three pieces of fillet, adjusting them as necessary to make the mitres join correctly in the corners. Wipe away any excess glue with a cotton bud and leave to dry overnight.

Make sure that the glass is still clean, then place the paper sculpture with mountboard and backing board in position, resting on the fillet all round. This should leave a comfortable margin at the back to fasten and seal the sandwich in position.

Set of medals

Another way of framing three-dimensional objects is to embed them partially or entirely in a backing so that they do not protrude and touch the glass. The ideal material to use for this is foam-core board, which is a layer of polystyrene foam between two layers of thin board. It makes a very lightweight backing into which holes can be cut to contain the objects that are being framed. The surface of the foam board is not particularly pleasant to look at, so it is usual to cover it – you can use a coloured mountboard with apertures cut to match exactly, or fabric which can be allowed to dip into the cavities.

Foam-core board is available in three thicknesses and I have chosen 5mm (¼in) for a project to frame a collection of medals and badges. Because of the thickness of the foam-core board I have to use a moulding with a rebate deep enough to contain everything: the foam, the backing board, a sheet of glass and also a narrow fillet to hold the glass so that it does not rest on the medals.

To mount and frame this collection of medals you will need a hockey-stick moulding with a rebate of about 25mm (1in), 5mm thick narrow fillet, a sheet of 5mm (¼in) thick foam-core board and a piece of thin silky fabric to tone with the medals. You will also need a piece of MDF and a sheet of glass.

Work out the size of the frame by arranging the medals on a spare piece of mountboard, moving them around until you have a satisfactory display. A symmetrical arrangement is usually more suitable for medals as it is most like the way that they would be worn on the uniform.

Make allowances for a title (if this is applicable) and allow for a border around the medals which is not too large; say 30mm (1^1/$_4$in): you do not want to have the medals isolated in a group in the middle with a lot of background all round. For this set of five medals and two badges my total area is 325 x 295mm (12^3/$_4$ x 11^5/$_8$in). Cut the foam, backing board and glass to these measurements.

Now trace out the rough outlines of each piece (including the ribbon and bars) and the position of the title on to the foam-core board in their required positions. It is worth taking a bit of time to map out the layout accurately and and also to double-check the measurements from each edge. Line up the separate medal ribbons with the tops of the three central ribbons to create a symmetry in the layout. Then arrange the shoulder flash in the centre with space left for the title card immediately below it.

Cut holes for the medals and the title using a scalpel or small craft knife: cut through the top layer of board, criss-cross the enclosed area with the blade and then dig out small pieces of foam. Cut through the bottom layer of board and lift it out. If your objects are not too deep, leave the bottom layer of board in place.

Alternatively, you can buy mount-cutters that are capable of cutting very small holes. Allow a little ease for the fabric, but avoid making the hole so large that the medal could move out of place.

Cut round the shapes required for the fastenings and pins, lift off the top layer of card and then dig a shallow recess into the foam so that the fastenings can be partially embedded in the foam.

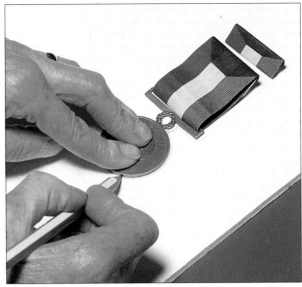

Draw the outline of each medal on the foam-core board.

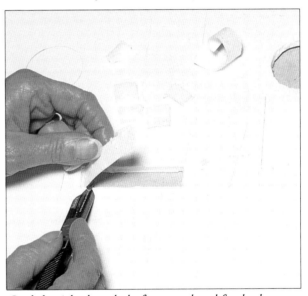

Cut holes right through the foam-core board for the deeper medals and for the title.

Dig out shallow recesses for fastenings and pins.

> **Framer's tip:** *When working with a set of objects which are different sizes and shapes it is worth taking time to map out the layout very accurately.*

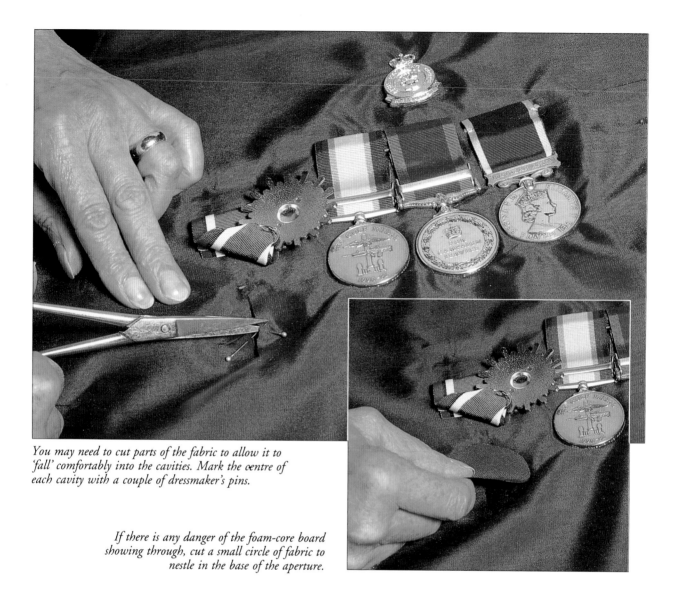

You may need to cut parts of the fabric to allow it to 'fall' comfortably into the cavities. Mark the centre of each cavity with a couple of dressmaker's pins.

If there is any danger of the foam-core board showing through, cut a small circle of fabric to nestle in the base of the aperture.

The piece of silky fabric needs to be considerably larger than the size of the foam-core board. Before you do any cutting, have a trial run, tucking it into all the cavities to see how it will lie.

When you are entirely satisfied that everything will lie correctly, iron the fabric and then immediately rearrange it on to the foam-core board.

If the pattern is simple you may be able to use the fabric without cutting it, but with a complicated pattern the fabric will probably not fall comfortably into all the cavities and will have to be cut.

Before you cut, mark the centre of each cavity with two dressmaker's pins so that you know exactly where your cuts must lie. Take great care when you cut the fabric and use very sharp scissors because on

no account must any of the cut edges show; keep the cuts quite small so that they are concealed under the medals. If you have an irregularly shaped medal and there is a danger that the white foam-core board might show through, cut a small circle of fabric to nestle into the base of the circular aperture.

Small dabs of glue are permissible in the bases of the shallow cavities, but do not put any glue on to the surface of the foam-core board in case it seeps through the thin fabric and marks it permanently.

You can now fold the excess fabric around the edges of the foam-core board and secure it on the back with pieces of masking tape. Again, it is worth taking time to do this whole process, as a skilful arrangement of fabric can really enhance the display.

Now secure each medal together with its ribbon in position. Again, you should not use glue, so try a reversible method.

Those items that have a small pin – the small ribbon bars, for example – can have the pin pushed through the foam and held in place with strips of masking tape on the back of the board, while fabric badges can be fastened with a couple of stitches made through the foam-core board. You can secure the actual medals with short lengths of wire, coiled around the link and pushed through to the back. The wires can be fastened to the back of the board with some more masking tape.

In this display of medals four had pins which could be poked into the foam-core board and three had small bars which could be secured from the back. If, in future years, you need to remove the medals from the frame, this will be very simple.

When the mount is finished, measure the total picture size again and then slip the mounted medals into a clean polythene bag to keep them clean until you are ready to complete the assembly. Cut your moulding, allowing 2mm (1/8in) ease, and make up the frame as usual. While the glue is setting, cut the fillets, as shown on page 55. Lay the frame face down on the workbench, clean your glass, place it in the frame and glue the fillets in position.

When the fillet joints are dry, place the mounted medals and the backing board into the frame so that they rest on the fillet. Do this with the frame in an upright position, rather than turning the mounted medals upside down.

Framer's Tip: When assembling any items that are free to move, stand the frame upright so that there is no chance of their slipping out of position. In fact, it is best to complete the frame in an upright position and then keep it that way until it is hung. This is a little difficult to do, but well worth while.

Push the ribbon-bar pins through the foam and then secure on the back with masking tape.

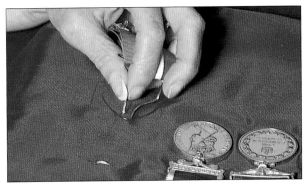
Use short lengths of wire to secure the actual medals.

Assemble the picture with the frame in the upright position.

Holding the glass away from the work: the finished three-dimensional paper sculpture from pages 54-55 in its special deep frame.

60

An alternative method is to recess the items to be framed. Here we have the completed set of medals and badges from pages 56-59.

24340754
CORPORAL BARRY HERMAN
ARMY CATERING CORPS.

3-D découpage is another craft that requires a deep-rebate frame and a fillet to keep the glass away from the work. In this case the mountboard is touching the glass and the 'fillets' are made from thin strips of foam-core board covered by mountboard glued to the inside edge of the aperture.

61

Box frames

When you want to frame a three-dimensional item which is more than about 50mm (2in) deep you have to be prepared to make a box frame for it, because there are no hockey-stick mouldings deep enough. Box frames can be made from a variety of different materials, depending on the weight of the item to be framed. A box for a very light item, such as a decorated egg, could be made from foam-core board covered with mountboard or fabric, but a more substantial item, such as this model boat, requires a more solid construction.

The box could be made from wood, plywood, thin· blockboard or chipboard. I did not want the wood to be too thick, which would have made the box very heavy, and knowing that I was going to paint the surfaces, I finally decided on 12mm ($\frac{1}{2}$in) chipboard. This is sturdy enough for the purpose, not too expensive and does not split in a warm room.

To make a box frame for this model boat I chose to use 12mm ($\frac{1}{2}$in) thick chipboard cut into 140mm (5$\frac{1}{2}$in) wide strips. When assembled the chipboard was treated with wood sealer and then painted. To complete the project you will also need a piece of 4mm ($\frac{1}{4}$in) plywood for the backing board, a piece of mountboard, some scrap lengths of MDF (to form the rebates at the front and back of the box), a sheet of glass and some flat beading to retain the glass. Finally, if you want to hang the box you will need four 25mm (1in) mirror plates.

You must also consider how the object will be fixed or held in the box. It is generally bad practice to glue an object to a surface, as this may detract from its value. One way is to suspend the object from the back of the box, and there is a range of holders manufactured for this purpose. However, in this case the boat will be standing on the base of the box on its own stand, which will be raised up on a block so that the boat will not be partially obscured by the beading. It is permissible to glue the stand to the block to hold the boat secure, but do not glue the boat to the stand.

Box frame for a model boat

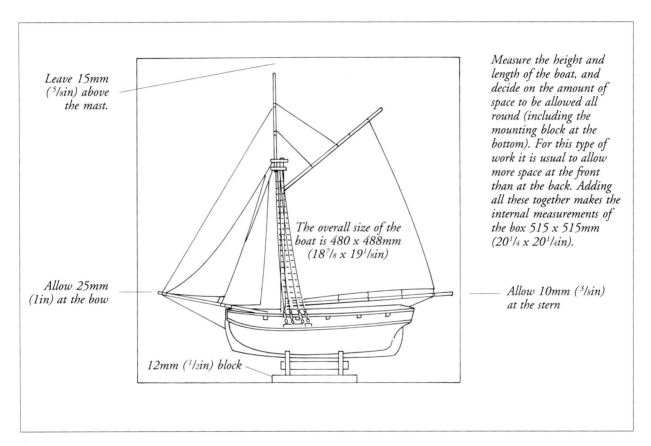

Leave 15mm (⁵/₈in) above the mast.

Measure the height and length of the boat, and decide on the amount of space to be allowed all round (including the mounting block at the bottom). For this type of work it is usual to allow more space at the front than at the back. Adding all these together makes the internal measurements of the box 515 x 515mm (20¹/₄ x 20¹/₄in).

The overall size of the boat is 480 x 488mm (18⁷/₈ x 19¹/₈in)

Allow 25mm (1in) at the bow

Allow 10mm (³/₈in) at the stern

12mm (¹/₂in) block

Stage one

Measure the height and length of the boat. Add space for the mounting block at the bottom and for some free space at the bow, the stern and the top of the mast (see diagram above) to find the internal measurements of the box. For this model these are 515 x 515mm (20¹/₄ x 20¹/₄in), a nice neat square.

Now measure the width of the boat and add thickness of the glass, the backing and mountboards and a minimum of free space at each side of the boat. For this box the total depth is 140mm (5¹/₂in). Rather than cut strips out of a large sheet of chipboard myself, I had them cut at the wood yard.

Stage two

Set your saw to 90° and cut two 515mm (20¼in) lengths from a strip of chipboard for the top and bottom; mark these T and B respectively. Now cut two more lengths, 539mm (21¼in) long – the internal height of the box plus twice the thickness of the chipboard; mark these L and R respectively. Cut a short 70mm (2¾in) length of chipboard for the mounting block.

Stage three

On each piece of chipboard measure and mark lines along its length, 2mm (¹/₁₆in) from one long edge and 10mm (³/₈in) from the other long edge.

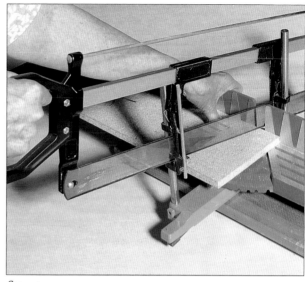

Stage two.

Stage four

Take the pieces marked L and R and lay them on a scrap of wood on the workbench with the ruled lines facing down. With a hammer, start four 30mm (1¼in) panel pins equally spaced and 6mm (¼in) from the short edge at each end. The panel pins need to be with their points just through the chipboard.

Arrange the pieces on the table in the positions shown in the sketch below, with all lines facing inwards and the 2mm (¹/₁₆in) ones at the top.

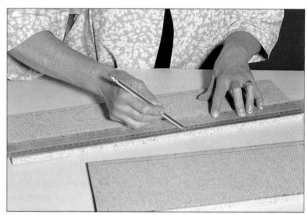

Stage three.

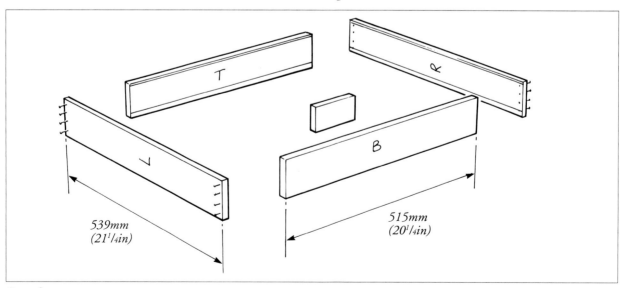

Stage four.

Stage five

Check the position of the drawn lines on the inside of the top (T) and left-hand-side (L) pieces of the box and then apply glue to one short edge of piece T. Stand T on end and balance L on top of it, supporting the other end of L on the bottom piece, B. Now carefully align the two pieces and hammer home the four panel pins.

Glue and nail the other three corners in a similar way and then put the box aside until the glue is completely dry.

Stage five.

Stage six

Now cut two pieces of MDF 515 x 128mm (20^1/$_4$ x 5in) and two pieces 511 x 128mm (20^1/$_8$ x 4^3/$_4$in) to form the rebate for the glass and backing board. Spread glue sparingly on one face of a long piece and stick it into the box on the bottom, carefully aligning it between the ruled lines. Allow the glue to set and repeat the process with the other long side, sticking it in the top of the box. Repeat the process with first one side piece and then the other.

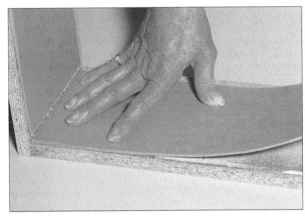

Stage six.

Stage seven

Stand the box flat on the workbench, put the boat, together with its stand, in the box and position it so that it looks attractive. Remember, it is preferable to have more space at the front, so the stand may not be central. When you are happy with the position, slip the mounting block underneath the stand. Carefully remove the boat, leaving the stand in place on the mounting block, and draw round the feet of the stand. Remove the stand and then draw round the mounting block.

Stage seven.

Stage eight
Remove the mounting block and, using a drill fitted with a 3.5mm (³/₁₆in) bit, drill two clearance holes within its rectangle on the bottom of the box. On the underside of the box, countersink the two holes. Replace the mounting block and, gripping it tightly in position, screw in two 20mm (³/₄in) x No. 6 countersunk wood screws from beneath.

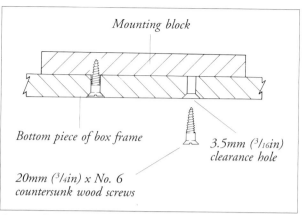

Mounting block

Bottom piece of box frame

20mm (³/₄in) x No. 6 countersunk wood screws

3.5mm (³/₁₆in) clearance hole

Stage eight.

Stage nine
Cut two 511 x 12mm (20¹/₈ x ¹/₂in) strips of MDF; these are to make a deeper rebate for the backing board at the sides. Turn the box so that its back is facing you, spread wood glue sparingly on one flat face of each piece and place one on each side lined up with the back edge of the MDF.

Stage nine.

Stage ten
Cut a 45° mitre on one end of the beading. Measure 539mm (21¹/₄in) along the outside edge of the beading and cut the second end. Check that it fits the box and then use it as a template for cutting the other three pieces.

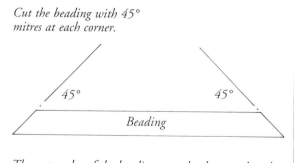

Cut the beading with 45° mitres at each corner.

45°   45°

Beading

The outer edge of the beading must be the same length as the external measurements of the box.

Stage ten.

Stage eleven

Treat the box and the four pieces of beading with wood seal to prevent the paint from soaking into the surface. Coat the inside and the outside of the box and the top of the beading. Do not paint the edges of the box, the four rectangles which mark the feet of the stand on the block and the underside of the beading. When the sealant is dry the box can be painted, again avoiding these areas.

You will probably have to apply at least two coats of paint and maybe three, making sure that one coat is completely dry before you paint the next. Lightly rub down with fine wire wool between each coat to improve the surface finish. On the final coat, paint a little way underneath the inside edge of the strips of beading to prevent any raw wood showing when the box is assembled.

Stage twelve

Screw the mirror plates on to the back edges of the box, positioning them so that they protrude beyond the sides of the box. I prefer to use four to be safe, although two may be adequate.

Stage thirteen

Lay the box flat on the workbench with the front, the 2mm (⅛in) border, facing you. Clean the glass and place it in the box resting on the MDF board ledge. Carefully apply wood glue to the edge of the box and then place the pieces of beading in position: align them with the outside edge of the box and match the mitres so that they fit exactly and overlap the glass. When the glue is dry, tap in three or four 12mm (½in) veneer pins equally spaced on each side and sink the heads using a nail set. Fill the indentations with tiny amounts of wood filler and touch up with paint when it is dry.

Stage eleven.

Stage twelve.

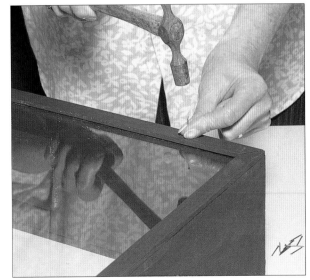

Stage thirteen.

Stage fourteen

Stand the box upright, apply wood glue to the four feet of the stand and place it on the marks on the mounting block in the box.

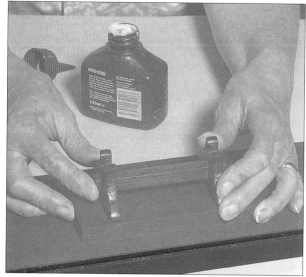

Stage fourteen.

Stage fifteen

Cut a 539mm (21^1/$_4$in) square from both the plywood and mountboard, glue the squares together using wood glue, and then put them under weights to dry.

The last stages of the assembly must be done carefully and with the box in the upright position because, of course, the boat is not fixed permanently on the stand.

Make sure the box is completely clean inside, place the boat in position on its stand and insert the backing board/mountboard sandwich in the back so that it rests on the ledges that were stuck into the back of the box. Fix the backing board in position with a brad gun or point driver or with hammer and nails. Gummed brown paper tape can be applied in the usual way to make a seal against dirt.

Stage fifteen.

Opposite: The finished box frame.

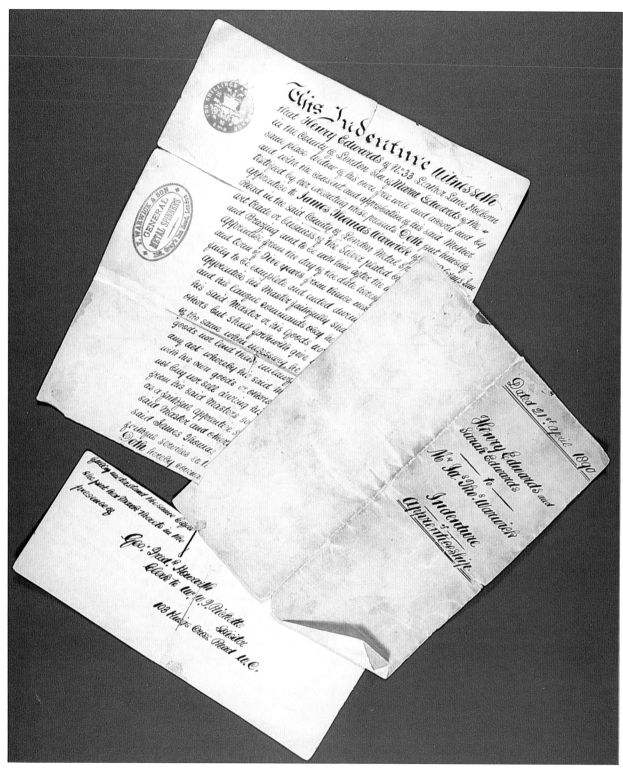

To frame this set of indentures you will need a moulding with a small 4mm (¹⁄₄in) rebate and some matching beading. I chose to use bare-faced materials which I stained with a dark oak colour and then polished with clear wax. You will also need two sheets of glass and some clear cellulose tape to seal the sandwich.

Double-sided frames

Occasionally you come across an item to be framed where it would be nice if you were able to see both sides. This can be a painting where the artist has used both sides of the paper, a piece of memorabilia or an item of family interest like the Indentures of 1890 that I am going to frame for this next project. It would be a shame to obscure one side of the document, because both sides are equally interesting and decorative, with the old copperplate writing and the seals. This old piece of paper has been folded for over 100 years and although two sections are missing this does not detract from its fascination, as, mercifully, they were the plain covers.

The way to frame this kind of subject is to set it between two pieces of glass instead of the normal glass and backing board. This means that provided that an appropriate hanger is used, it could be hung either way round on the wall, or suspended as part of a room divider. The trick is to carefully select a

moulding with a small rebate of only 4mm (^{1}/$_4$in), which is one you would normally avoid, because it is too small to contain the normal sandwich, but it is ideal for this purpose.

The back is secured by a piece of beading which is stained or painted to match the frame, so it is also important to choose a plain moulding that is not too difficult to match, or to make the frame in a bare-faced moulding so that everything can be stained the same colour. I have decided on this latter option, but I will use a dark-oak stain which will be appropriate to the age of the document.

The subject could be framed with no borders and the frame set to the edges, but most things look far more attractive if a clear border of glass is left around them. When the picture is hung, the colour of the wall or the wallpaper will make a border or, if it is made into part of a room divider, the subject will look as if it is suspended in space.

Framing a document

A border will set this document off and I suggest allowing 30mm (1^1/$_4$in) all round, making the total picture size 482 x 390mm (19 x 15^3/$_8$in).

Cut the moulding into four pieces for the frame, allowing 2mm (^{1}/$_8$in) ease, and make up in the usual way. Measure the outside edges of the frame and cut the beading to these sizes with 45° corners that fit exactly on to the back of the frame. Stain and wax all the pieces and make up the frame in the normal way.

Make the frame and then cut four pieces of beading.

Find the centre of one long side of the frame, align a wreath-top hanger with the edge of the moulding, mark the shape with a pencil and then, using a chisel or craft knife, cut out a recess just deep enough to take the thickness of the wreath-top hanger. Fasten the hanger in place using two small screws (you may find it easier to start the holes with a bradawl).

Thoroughly clean both sides of both sheets of glass and place the document on one sheet. Make sure that the pieces are all in their proper places and that the borders are equal all round. Immediately sandwich it with the other sheet of glass but on no account use glue to fasten it in place because the process must be reversible. On one side of this sandwich, carefully align a strip of narrow cellulose tape 2mm ($^1/_8$in) in from the edge of the top sheet of glass. Rub it down and then lap the overhang round the two thicknesses of glass and on to the bottom sheet. Repeat this process on the remaining three sides. This will hold the two sheets, and the enclosed document, firmly together, as well as providing a seal against dirt and flies.

Place the sandwich in the frame with the wreath-top hanger at the top, sparingly apply wood glue to the back face of the frame and place the four pieces of beading in line with the edges of the frame so that their mitres fit exactly.

Allow the glue to dry completely, then tap in four 10mm ($^3/_8$in) panel pins on the top edge, placing one either side of the wreath-top hanger. However, two panel pins will be sufficient on the other three sides of the frame. All the pin heads must be recessed with a nail set, filled and touched up with stain and wax.

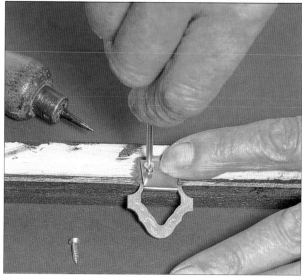

Screw a wreath-top hanger centrally in the top of the frame.

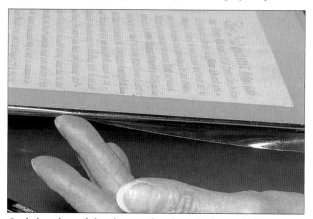

Seal the edges of the glass sandwich with clear cellulose tape.

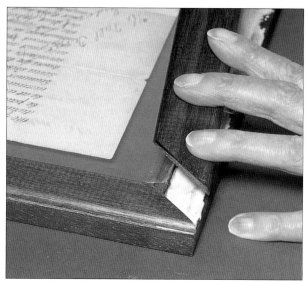

Glue the pieces of beading to the back of the moulding.

The two sides of the finished framed document.

Fancy cutting

If you want to create a really spectacular effect, some non-rectangular frames will be very eye-catching, especially if they are hung in a group. They are particularly suitable for floral paintings or pressed flowers, lace, old photographs or miniatures. Most saws of the type we are using in this book have the angles for five-, six- and eight-sided frames marked on the base, which makes it fairly simple to cut these shapes; the only decision that has to be made is about the length of the sides.

The sides of the frame do not all have to be the same length, so you can, for example, make an elongated octagon which will be suitable for a full-length mirror. You can be even more adventurous, and make diamonds, gem shapes, fan shapes or almost anything else you can dream up.

One thing to remember with all fancy cutting is that you get more waste when cutting angles other than 45°, and, usually, you will need more moulding than for the conventional four-sided frame. However, it is sometimes possible to use up offcuts from another project where you made a set of matching frames.

You can buy charts that give tables of the length moulding has to be cut to relate to a particular picture size. These charts show frames with different numbers of sides and of different shapes, and are a very useful addition to the workshop.

Most band clamps have corner pieces that can be used for different angles, but sometimes you will want one that is not there. In this case, use the nearest shape and equalise the space at either side.

Set of pressed flowers

When working with fancy shapes make some rough sketches of possible arrangements – experiment with shape and grouping. For this set of pressed and mounted flowers I have decided to make a group of different-shaped frames, using the same design of moulding but in a selection of different colourways to link with the colour schemes in the flowers.

This arrangement includes a six-sided frame (a hexagon), a pair of five-sided frames (pentagons), an elongated five-sided frame (Christmas-tree shape) and a pair of elongated four-sided frames (tear-drop shapes). The six frames are to be hung as a group, so I will not make any of them too large. For this project, the six-sided frame has a picture area of 205mm (8in) across the hexagon and the others are worked in proportion.

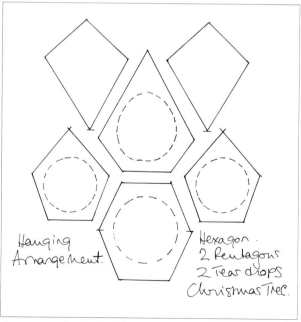

Draw a rough sketch of the arrangement.

When making a group presentation of a set of images, such as these pressed-flower pictures, you could use bare-faced mouldings (either the same or different profiles) and then paint or stain them to suit the colour scheme. For this set I used different colourways of the same design of finished mouldings. You will also need a selection of coloured mountboards and some glass.

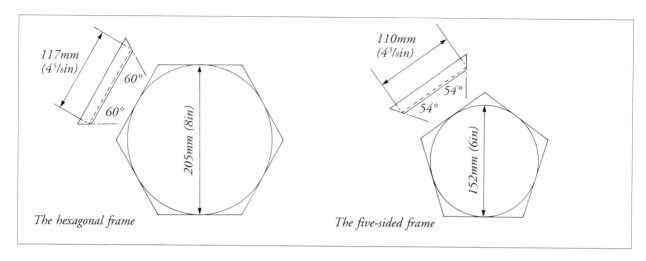

The hexagonal frame

The five-sided frame

Hexagonal frame

Draw a hexagon around a circle 205mm (8in) in diameter as shown above and you will find that you will need six pieces of moulding each measuring 117mm (4⁵/₈in), with a 60° mitre on each end.

Cut one end of the moulding, measure along the inside of the rebate and then cut the other end. Use this master as a template for the other five pieces.

Expand the band clamp and turn the corners for a six-sided frame (the 60° angle). Make up the frame as usual, but take care when tightening the clamp to ensure that none of the joints slip out of position. Clean off excess glue with a cotton bud.

When the frame is complete, use it as a template for cutting the glass. You can either cut this yourself or take the frame to the glass cutter. Use the cut glass as a template for cutting the backing board – draw round the glass and cut on the inside of the lines. To ensure accuracy I suggest that you redraw the shape on the back of the mountboard and then cut it out. Turn the board over, mark the centre of the hexagon and use this mark to cut a circular aperture.

Five-sided frames

For a pentagon the angles are 54° and in this case I want a 152mm (6in) nominal picture area, which makes the length of the sides 110mm (4³/₈in). For a pair of frames you must cut ten pieces to this length.

If your band clamp does not have corners to fit a five-sided frame, use the 60° corners and equalise the spaces either side of each joint. Assemble the frames in the normal way. Again, cut the glass, backing board and mountboard as for the hexagonal frame.

Most mitre saws have symbols to help you set the correct angles for five-, six- and eight-sided frames.

If your band clamp does not have 54° corners, use the 60° ones and equalise any space either side of each joint.

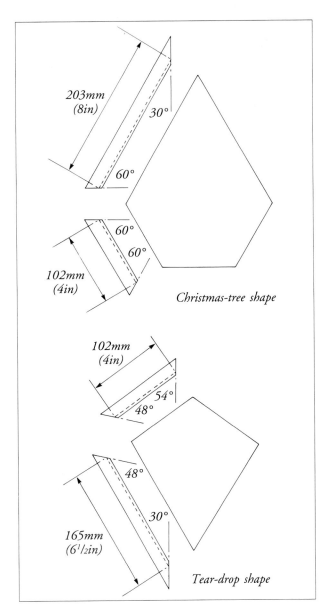

203mm
(8in)   30°

60°

60°

60°

102mm
(4in)

Christmas-tree shape

102mm
(4in)

54°
48°

48°

30°

165mm
(6¹/₂in)

Tear-drop shape

remember to cut the mouldings as a handed pair.

Again, you need a little ingenuity to use your corner blocks on the band clamp, and I suggest that you position the 30° angle in the corner piece that is set in the body of the clamp.

It will also be more awkward to pin these angles, so take care, particularly on the sharp corner.

Teardrop-shaped frames

Teardrop (or extended-diamond) frames have a combination of three angles, with 54° at the top, 48° at the sides and 30° at the sharp point. For this particular pair of frames the short sides measure 102mm (4in) and the long sides 165mm (6¹/₂in).

Make them up as you did the Christmas-tree-shaped frame.

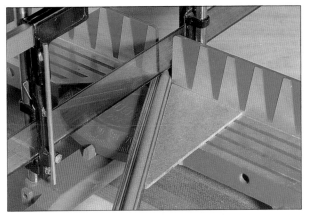

Set the saw to 90° and use a 30/60° template to cut a 30° angle for the Christmas-tree and tear-drop-shaped frames.

Take care when pinning the corners of fancy-shaped frames.

Christmas-tree-shaped frame

A Christmas-tree shape has five sides: three of one length and two of another. The sharp-pointed angle at the top is 30° and the other four angles are 60° as in the six-sided frame. The long sides are 203mm (8in) and the three short sides are 102mm (4in).

Cut the moulding in much the same way as before, but use a small scrap of MDF cut as a 30/60° template. Set the saw at 90°, position the template against the back support, align the moulding against the template and cut the acute 30° angle. When pieces of moulding have different angles at each end, and you require a left-hand and a right-hand piece,

The finished arrangement of fancy frames.

INDEX